ACTING EXERCISES FOR
NON-TRADITIONAL STAGING

Acting Exercises for Non-Traditional Staging: Michael Chekhov Reimagined offers a new set of exercises for coaching actors when working on productions that are non-traditionally staged in arenas, thrusts, or alleys. All of the exercises are adapted from Michael Chekhov's acting technique, but are reimagined in new and creative ways that offer innovative twists for the practitioner familiar with Chekhov, and easy accessibility for the practitioner new to Chekhov. Exploring the methodology through a modern-day lens, these exercises are energizing additions to the classroom and essential tools for more a vibrant rehearsal and performance.

Anjalee Deshpande Hutchinson is an Associate Professor of Theatre & Dance and the Department Chair at Bucknell University. She is a National Michael Chekhov Association Certified Teacher.

ACTING EXERCISES FOR NON-TRADITIONAL STAGING

MICHAEL CHEKHOV REIMAGINED

Anjalee Deshpande Hutchinson

Routledge
Taylor & Francis Group

NEW YORK AND LONDON

First published 2018
by Routledge
711 Third Avenue, New York, NY 10017

and by Routledge
2 Park Square, Milton Park, Abingdon, Oxon OX14 4RN

Routledge is an imprint of the Taylor & Francis Group, an informa business

Library of Congress Cataloging-in-Publication Data
Names: Hutchinson, Anjalee Deshpande, author.
Title: Acting exercises for non-traditional staging : Michael Chekhov reimagined /
    Anjalee Deshpande Hutchinson.
Description: New York and London : Routledge, 2017. | Includes bibliographical
    references and index.
Identifiers: LCCN 2017000649 | ISBN 9781138236257 (hbk : alk. paper) |
    ISBN 9781138236264 (pbk : alk. paper) | ISBN 9781315271163 (ebk : alk. paper)
Subjects: LCSH: Acting—Handbooks, manuals, etc.
Classification: LCC PN2061 .H88 2017 | DDC 792.02/8—dc23
LC record available at https://lccn.loc.gov/2017000649

ISBN: 978-1-138-23625-7 (hbk)
ISBN: 978-1-138-23626-4 (pbk)
ISBN: 978-1-315-27116-3 (ebk)

Typeset in Bembo
by Apex CoVantage, LLC

Visit the companion website: www.routledge.com/cw/hutchinson

For Mala. For Annapurna. For Emily S. For Nicholas James.
And of course for Misha.
May his words and teachings continue to light the
way for years to come.

CONTENTS

FOREWORD

Perhaps Michael Chekhov's greatest gift to teachers of his technique is that of freedom. He specifically encourages us to identify the challenge that needs solving or the lesson we wish to share and then create our own exercises to fill that objective. Anjalee Deshpande Hutchinson has taken his gift of freedom and done just this over the past decade. Now she shares with us her developments with a focus on what I believe is an under-addressed subject: how the form of the stage changes the actor's job.

Together with her contributing colleagues, Hutchinson has reimagined Mr. Chekhov's approach for you, specifically to answer the questions "What else must an actor develop to meet the specifics of Non-traditional Staging and Production? How can we help them do that?"

Whether you are already a Michael Chekhov teacher or new to his ideas, you will find this book useful. While the book requires of us no previous in-depth exposure to Mr. Chekhov, I discovered delightful twists and fresh perspectives on some tried and true exercises that have me "jonesing" to get into the classroom to explore. I want to play as an actor and a teacher. I am wonderfully curious to guide and witness other actors' responses and growth. I foresee the skill sets that are built with these exercises becoming evermore critical for the actor.

Mr. Chekhov was devoted to an image of the Theatre of the Future and what it would offer its audiences. Non-traditional Staging and Performance is part of that future and our present. Indeed Hutchinson reminds us that non-traditional stages are really throwbacks to the past, the very origins of performance. And so we ask: What must theatre bring to the spectator? What did it once bring, that has been lost?

What will it need to bring more than ever? Who must the artist be, in order to achieve that?

To answer those questions, we must also ask: Who is the spectator of the future? I have heard that seventy percent of people surveyed said they would rather have their phone with them on a vacation than their significant other. The young audiences are lost between reality and a screen, yearning for connection with life. The upside is that, to get that connection, people will now pay as much as two thousand dollars for one ticket to a Broadway show. This bodes well for all live performances, if they can meet the increasing gap between vitality and "digitality."

Non-traditional Staging offers ideal forms to create an intimate connection with the audience that surpasses what can be "cheated out" on a proscenium stage. It calls for different training. We need 360° communication to raise the bar of live performance.

This digital epidemic is leading to our future actors arriving in the classroom with very narrow fields of focus, primarily from the frontal space, with digitally oriented bits of information pouring from their heads. They will have strong concentration skills in a tunnel vision of multitasking. Their bodies will be outside their tunnels, floundering, with the creative impulse only able to move their thumbs. Many teachers are seeing this already.

Mr. Chekhov's approach, with its emphasis on full psychophysical expression, trains any actor for any medium and style. Through the following pages, all actors can build the awareness, concentration and imaginative skill sets to become 360° actors. Thus, in proscenium or arena, alley or thrust, the playground of ideas here is highly practical for actors, teachers and directors.

Ms. Hutchinson's unique perspective offers us an opportunity to expand our own way of viewing. She uses Chekhov's idea of "baptizing" or "giving a name to something" to help us discover rich images associated with concepts we may well know under more familiar terms. In re-baptizing some classic exercises, Hutchinson allows us to engage anew, to reimagine Chekhov through the Non-traditional Staging lens and beyond. Her book comes at the perfect time.

Lisa Loving Dalton
President of the National Michael
Chekhov Association

PREFACE

This is a book of acting exercises for use in academic and professional theatre. All these exercises are based on the work of Michael Chekhov and the Michael Chekhov acting technique. The exercises were selected to be included in this text because they are particularly useful for productions staged in the round, thrust, alley or site specific. All of the exercises are 'riffs' on Michael Chekhov's original methodology. Obviously nothing can replace the original masterworks *To the Actor* and *On the Technique of Acting* by Michael Chekhov, but the exercises in this book offer a new way in for the beginner and an expansion of the repertoire for the master practitioner.

I have been teaching and directing at the collegiate level for 20 years. For the last 10 of those years I have been employing the Michael Chekhov Technique. When I took my first MC workshop as a young actor/director/professor, it was because I had read about the technique and wanted to find some exercises to integrate into my acting class as a complement to the more standard Stanislavski methodology which had been the focus of my actor training in the United States. I saw a mailing from the National Michael Chekhov Association about a summer workshop and thought I would give it a try. What I found was so much more than a set of exercises to add to the toolbox. I found a stronger more comprehensive way to build character, engage the imagination and build community. I found this to be true when I returned in the fall both with my classes and, to my great delight, in my rehearsals. I began to engage with the student actors in a whole new way. I found the Chekhov Technique to be incredibly useful for myself as a director, performer and theatre artist as well as an educator.

As a theatre academic in a liberal arts institution, I have looked far and wide for ways to make performance more readily accessible to majors and non-majors alike, as well as those who teach and direct majors and non-majors. The Chekhov Technique has been the most successful way I have found to connect to actors with varying levels of experience, training and confidence. My approach to this connection is playful. This book is the culmination of years of play, as a director, as a teacher and as a theatre artist. What has emerged over the course of time are 'new takes' on the brilliant ideas of the Master, and new ways to look at his original concepts from a modern global point of view.

In addition the results of my own Chekhov 'experiments' over the years, included in this book are the experiments and experience of many professional experts in the field of performance in Non-Traditional Performance Spaces. Some are professionals who have worked for years on the arena stage. Others are professors with 30 years' experience on the thrust. Included also are designers: a lighting designer, a costume designer and a set designer—all with extensive experience in non-traditional spaces. Some of these experts are familiar with the Michael Chekhov Technique, some are not. Regardless, they all have valuable information to share on non-traditional staging and performance and their essays are included at the end of each chapter to supplement the work at hand.

In addition, I have also included in each chapter the works of two extraordinary master teachers: Wil Kilroy and Samantha Norton. Wil Kilroy is the vice president of the National Michael Chekhov Association and has been training actors, directors and teachers for 30 years. Wil's exercises are included here to offer more breadth and depth to the text. Samantha Norton is an actress with a degree in opera and vocal technique, as well as a certified fight choreographer. Her vocal exercises are included here in order to bring a more in-depth physically vocal component to the work. Both master teachers offer delightful new approaches and strong methodology to give readers the best foundation for non-traditional staging, performance and the exploration of the Michael Chekhov Technique.

ACKNOWLEDGMENTS

I have invented nothing. All of the exercises in this book are adaptations, re-imaginings and re-interpretations of the exercises of the master actor and acting teacher Michael Chekhov, who died long before I was born. Yet they are also riffs off all the exercises created by the excellent teachers and mentors I have had the great joy of working with across the years.

Although I cannot mention them all, here are the ones to whom I owe particular thanks and all my gratitude: the late wonderful Mala Powers, Lisa Dalton, Wil Kilroy, Joanna Merlin, David Zinder, Lenard Petit, Jessica Cerullo, Bud Beyer, Ed Menta and Bill Morris. Profound thanks also to Michael Kass and Rev. Ed Oberholtzer on the secrets of breathwork and meditation, and to Rich Brown and Andy Paris for our work in devised and experimental theatre. Palace of Gratitude thanks to Lisa Loving Dalton for helping me make sense of the text, Samantha Norton and Wil Kilroy for offering amazing exercises, Pablo Guerra-Monje for the wonderful illustrations, Gordon Wenzel who shot gorgeous photos of our workshops and all of the brilliant essay contributors who made this book complete. Extra special thanks to the actors who took part in the workshop and whose shining faces and beautiful work illustrate this book so wonderfully: Alex Wade, Casey Venema, Favour Unigwe, Gabe Calleja, Greg Wolf, Guelmi Espinosa, Huthaifa Aladwan, Kat Swank, Kate Donithan, Kate Franklin, Kyle Cohick, Liana Irvine, Midge Zuk, Mukta Phatak, Rodney West and Dustyn Martincich.

Humble thanks to all the acting and directing professors from whom I have taken workshops and found inspiration at the Association for

Theatre in Higher Education conferences across the years. Big thanks to my collaborators in the Bucknell Department of Theatre and Dance and to all my colleagues and mentors at Bucknell for the generous encouragement on my journey.

Crazy gratitude to Stacey Walker and Meredith Darnell, my wonderful collaborators at Routledge and to Annie Martin, my inside woman in publishing who gave me the courage to make this happen! Extra special thanks to my parents Ashok and Asha Deshpande for supporting my theatrical pursuit when it was uncommon for Indian parents in America to do so, and to my wonderful husband Mark (Hutch) Hutchinson and all of our kids—Coe, Kate, Akash (Koosh) and Ketaki (Kiya)—for putting up with mom while she was putting together this book. Lastly, many constellations of thanks to my students across the years who have filled my life and life's work with magic and delight. I am constantly astonished by your strength and grace.

Blood Wedding by Federico Garcia Lorca, adapted by Caridad Svich. Alley-style production directed by Anjalee Deshpande Hutchinson, lighting design by Heath Hansum, set design by F. Elaine Williams, costume design by Jenny Kenyon. Bucknell University 2009.

Credit: Enche Tjin

Credit: drawing courtesy of Pablo Guerra-Monje

1

AN INTRODUCTION: GETTING COMFY WITH THE WEIRD STUFF

What Do We Mean by 'Non-Traditional Staging and Performance'?

If you would have asked me that question 25 years ago, I probably would have answered, 'the weird stuff.' My first experience with theatre was at the Fisher Theatre in Detroit. I saw a touring production of *Annie* with my father when I was 11 years old. I adored it. Then I saw *Les Miserables*, *Phantom of the Opera* and *Cats*, all touring productions over the next few years. I ate them up. I got involved with middle school and high school theatre, drama camps and community theatre. By the time I was accepted to undergrad, I figured I was something of an expert. Yeah, exactly. I was *that* student. You know the one. The first time I visited the college I would eventually spend the next four years at, I noticed one of their main stage spaces was somewhat different than what I was used to, it was not a box with a frame around it. It was not a proscenium. It was a thrust. I was put off. I thought it was a bit 'hippy.' I mean I knew they did weird stuff in the sixties but that wasn't the theatre of today! Wouldn't the audience on one side feel cheated? Can't they just do normal shows?

Up until that point, I had never seen any theatre performed on a stage outside of a proscenium stage. That is because the great majority of popular Western theatre in this century has been staged in a proscenium-style stage space. It is usually our first exposure to theatre unless we are lucky enough to live in a place like New York or Chicago or Atlanta where other kinds of spaces prevail. Even then, you'd need to have had some very cultured parents who knew enough about theatre to seek out the more innovative productions and production spaces. The proscenium stage, although not really traditional in the historic sense of the word, is our inherited traditional legacy here in America.

When I refer to non-traditional staging and performance, I am referring to productions that are staged in the round/arena (where the audience is seated all around the stage which could be a square, circle, triangle, etc.), or on a thrust (where the audience is seated on three sides of the performance and the stage juts out a bit beyond the apron of the proscenium), or in an alley (where the audience is seated on two opposing sides of the performance—across from each other) or site-specific (which could be anywhere—many floors of a warehouse, a garden, a pit, a bridge, an abandoned asylum, a corporate high rise, etc.) But the term, 'non-traditional' is sort of a lie. The term is a misnomer. It would be more correct to call these types of productions 'ultra-traditional.'

One can assume that before recorded history, theatre was storytelling—and storytelling in many early cultures was done around a communal fire. One of the first recorded histories of Western theatre dates back to 6th century BC. This theatre, one of the first theatres of the Greeks, is believed to have been in the round. Akin to sitting around a campfire, the circular theatre was an homage to a kind of circular dance of life, where the chorus sang and danced in response to the actors performing

'Communal Fire.' *Macbeth* by William Shakespeare, directed by Anjalee Deshpande Hutchinson, set design by F. Elaine Williams, lighting design by Heath Hansum, costume design by Paula Davis. Bucknell University 2008. Credit: Mark Hutchinson

in the inner ring of the stage. Later in the 4th century, the shape became more of a semi-circle, where the audience sat on a hill watching the action on a wooden stage. By the 3rd century, the semi-circle remained complemented by raked stone seating but still out in the open air.

Meanwhile, in another part of the world, one of the earliest texts about Eastern theatre practice is the *Natya Shastra* by Bharata written sometime between 500 and 200 BC. In this text, three kinds of theatre spaces are described: square, rectangle and triangle. Although all are setup in a somewhat proscenium style, the author did describe in great detail that theatres should be small and intimate, and that the largest kinds of theatre were reserved only for the Gods. Humans would not be able to comprehend the stories told in the largest theatres (interesting when we connect this idea to William Shakespeare's iconic quote, 'All the World's a Stage', the world being an incomprehensible place sometimes). One of the earliest recorded styles of theatre was Japanese Noh, which was performed in a kind of obtuse L-shape where a bridge-way led to a platform and the audience was seated to one side of the 'L'. Noh theatre also used a chorus, who sat at the side of the stage and sang, recited or played the music that told the story that the main characters enacted onstage. Kabuki also made use of the L-shape. This style enjoyed a shallow proscenium arch stage that was connected to the back of the auditorium by a raised bridge called a hanamichi. Drama was enacted on both the stage and the hanamichi.

Elizabethan theatre in the 17th century was influenced by classical Greek theatre and was often characterized by three tiers of wooden seating in a semi-circle around a wooden stage. The Globe Theatre in London, England (built at the turn of the century in 1599 which the modern replica is based on) is a perfect example of this kind of structure. Before long, there was a huge shift in world politics, which resulted in a transformation for the theatre. This change began in England. Back in the first days of the Globe when Queen Elizabeth was in power, the aristocrats and the commoners all shared in the experience of the performance, theatre was for everyone. During the reign of Charles I, there were more and more private theatres, which catered to the rich. Then during the English civil war in 1642, all theatre was banned in London and for 18 years there was a general assault against theatre in all forms all over England. The mind frame of the puritanical protestant authorities regarded theatre as being pagan and dangerous, citing the avarice of the romans from which it was born.

'Pagan and Dangerous.' *The Bacchae*; devised production adapted from Euripides, directed by Anjalee Deshpande Hutchinson, set design by Jenny Kenyon, costume design by Paula Davis, Lighting Design by Heath Hansum. Bucknell University 2011.

Credit: Mark Hutchinson

When the monarchy was restored in 1660 by Charles II, theatres reopened, but the popular style of the time came as a swing of the pendulum with bawdy restoration comedies. Although the productions were open to all, the sexual explicitness and general morality in the plays reflected a taste expressed in patriarchal aristocratic circles, not in the general public. This type of play was a favorite of Charles II, who had enjoyed these kinds of shows in other parts of Europe when he was away during the war, and he encouraged the English adaptation of the form when he returned. The mind frame expressed by the puritan-ical protestant authorities remained with the general public. Gradually more and more theatres could only remain open if they began catering specifically to the rich. The experience of theatre to be enjoyed by the masses began to lose steam, first in England, then across Europe.

What we consider the modern-day 'traditional' proscenium arch that you see in most Broadway, regional and community theatres, as well as in most high school auditoriums, wasn't really 'invented' until around the late 17th century in Europe. The raised platform was created with an arch around the front to simulate the illusion of a frame. This was in part a reflection of the needs of innovative new forms of theatre known as Neoclassical, Melodrama and eventually Realism. In the neoclassical form, the idea was to create theatre on a larger scale: intricate, grand and elaborate. In melodrama, illusion was key, the ability to provoke excitement through thrills and action! In realism, a different kind of illusion took hold. The utilization of the 'the fourth wall' was created to allow audiences the ability to peer into other people's lives without them knowing. As you can imagine, this was *super* popular. Everyone wanted to be a spy into other people's lives. Exciting!

At the same time, theatre architecture and interior design continued to grow more ornate with richly detailed gilded ceilings and velvet seating. Ticket prices went up and much of Western theatre settled into becoming the main pastime of the wealthy. But as the form evolved from restoration into neoclassical, melodrama and finally into realism, it stayed away from the more visceral components of the kinds of theatre that came before. Sure, there were always the exceptions (symbolism, expressionism, etc.) but the majority of popular Western theatre became locked into the tastes of the rich. The wealthy were not interested in the kind of theatre that came before, they did not want the actors too close or to have to be involved in a way in which they were not comfortable. In short, they didn't want to work. They wanted to be entertained! This kind of theatre took hold of the modern world and became the most popular form of theatre from that point to this very day.

Yet something was lost in the transition. When going to the theatre became an expensive endeavor beholden to the whims of the wealthy, a kind of intimacy between performer and audience was lost. The audience became comfortable witnessing a play rather than experiencing it. Experiencing a play asks more from an audience and it is more difficult than just watching. Watching allows an audience to sit back and observe actors from a safe distance. Ever have a relative say, 'that was very nice' about a play you were in? That usually means they were at a 'safe distance' emotionally, intellectually and/or spiritually. Experiencing a play means being connected to the performance in a more visceral way. The audience has to be up for it. The audience has to want it. By the time realism began to grow, it became more common for audiences to disengage with experiencing performances in an active way and the clear delineation between audience and performer was created.

This was a huge disconnect from the more experiential theatre of the past. All the way from the time of the early Greeks to the theatre of the Elizabethans (and even longer in much of the Eastern world), a play was not a set of scenes to be watched alone, isolated in the dark but a story/ritual to be experienced with community. So how is that different? It is the difference between watching a televangelist on TV and actually going to church with your family. It is the difference between watching *Star Wars* on your laptop in your room or going to the movie's premiere at midnight with some friends and a whole bunch of strangers, all dressed up as Han Solo, Princess Leia or Chewbacca. It is the difference between liking an Instagram photo of a friend at a wedding or actually going to that wedding and laughing with that friend or a bunch of your best friends. One is nice; the other is *so much more*. It is fulfilling or resonant or meaningful in powerful ways. Getting all your camping gear together, taking time off work, arranging everything with your friends—these are not 'easy.' But actually going makes all the difficulty worth it.

We have become a culture that is comfortable with convenience rather than a culture that seeks fulfillment. You know the latter is better than the former but actually doing it means you've got to battle your own inertia. Most people give up the battle before even starting. Some people don't even know they are missing out. You know that

'The Instagram Shot.' *Five Women Wearing the Same Dress* by Alan Ball, directed by Anjalee Deshpande Hutchinson, set design by F. Elaine Williams, costume design by Paula Davis, lighting design by Heath Hansum. Bucknell University 2009. Credit: Mark Hutchinson

great feeling of time spent doing something fun, something new or even something hard with someone whose company you enjoy? How about if that someone is new? How about when it's a group of people? Now compare that to noticing that you just killed an hour looking at Facebook and now feel kind of 'yuck.' Not bad exactly. Just not good. Maybe like everyone is having a better time than you. Or maybe that everything is so superficial and nothing feels important. Or like you are becoming a sloth. And somehow this feels more comfortable than actually calling (or even texting) your friend and arranging to do something fun? Oftentimes even if we get that far, the 'something fun' involves more watching, less doing. Many of us would rather go to the movies after a hard week than try to arrange and go on a hike. Right?

And yet so many of us are longing for *so much more*. And this is where theatre can make a difference. *Non-traditional staging*, as we explore in this book, is an audience/performer connection that demands more than a unique configuration of staging or space. It demands *non-traditional performance technique*. It is about creating an experience for your audience that is more intimate, more resonant, more meaningful.

I am not saying that traditionally staged/presented theatre cannot often be fun, entertaining, moving or thought-provoking. I am saying that non-traditional staging and performance leans into what theatre is best at: the intentionally intimate shared experience. Film has a hard time creating a communal experience. Film is much better at realistic voyeurism—which is why the film industry is doing so much better than the theatre industry, because film creators are leaning into the medium's strengths. When theatre makers lean into theatre's strengths—those good 'old fashioned' ways of connecting to the audience—we allow the experience of performance to open new doors of meaning and revelation for our audiences and for ourselves. It often takes more expense and effort on the part of the audience to experience theatre than it does to experience film, so what is it that audiences get in return? Spectacle is great but in order for theatre to thrive, audiences need and want more. Non-traditional stagings offer a way to do that, a way to breathe the same air as the performers, to palpably feel the energy on stage and to give that energy back through focused attention, and to respond as a part of a community experiencing a story together.

Who Was Michael Chekhov?

Whenever I begin teaching Chekhov Technique anew, I always have a few students who confuse Michael Chekhov with Anton Chekhov, who was Michael Chekhov's uncle. Anton Chekhov was of course the famous Russian playwright who wrote *The Seagull*, *Three Sisters*, *Uncle Vanya* and many other well-known classics. Anton Chekhov was born in 1860, died in 1904 and worked almost exclusively with master director and acting teacher Konstantin Stanislavski. Michael Chekhov (1891–1955) was one of Stanislavski's actors, a part of his acting troupe and was reported to be a favorite of the legendary director. Stanislavski trained Michael Chekhov and Chekhov in turn became one of Stanislavski's best students at the first incarnation of the Moscow Arts Theatre. A favorite not because he was his colleague's nephew and had most likely grown up in and around the theatre, but because he had an exceptional ability to embody Stanislavski's method and fully become someone else onstage.

The extent of his extraordinary talent was palpable to audiences, ensembles and directors alike. He embodied 'It.' The 'It' that makes performers mesmerizing onstage, hard to look away from. The 'It' that sometimes makes them appear taller, brighter, youthful or more

Michael Chekhov.
Credit: National Michael Chekhov Association

experienced and oftentimes much more vibrant on stage than off. I am sure you have either seen or known some of those actors. The kind of actor that gives off something visceral, something deeply resonant and moving when they perform.

Although many scholars often speak about the rifts between Chekhov and his mentor Stanislavski, Lisa Loving Dalton, one of the leading scholars of Chekhov Technique and Michael Chekov's history, states that rather than rifts, the two had a unique friendship and a mutual admiration:

> In the mid 1910's, Chekhov had upset Stanislavski, when, as a student, he acted out an affective memory "private moment" that no one had seen. This is a famous Stanislavski exercise where you develop the skill to do private behavior in public, also known as public solitude. In it, you are supposed to act out a moment from your real life that you haven't ever told anyone about. Chekhov acted out the death of his father—with not a dry eye in the house. Stanislavski lauded his work, pointing to it as evidence of the power of this approach. The problem was that Chekhov's dad was still alive! So how could Chekhov do that through imagination only? Why did he escape to imagination? Was it his dreadful, dysfunctional, abused upbringing that caused this? Out of the Moscow Art Theatre, "Mischa" was kicked—expelled for an "overheated imagination." The problem with expulsion quickly cleared, because this young man was a superstar, and the theatre needed him. Stanislavski remained a true advocate of Chekhov's throughout the tumultuous career that followed.
>
> Mikhail Chekhov, Mischa, grew to be renowned throughout Russia, and revered by all who met him. He is to this day considered the greatest actor ever to have blessed the Russian stage. Yet, Mischa did enter a period of deep psycho-spiritual crisis, even walking off the stage mid-performance. Rather than firing him, Stanislavski personally paid for Chekhov's psychiatric treatment and saved his place at the theatre for when he became well enough again to act. Interestingly, this crisis was resolved when Chekhov found an entirely new definition of himself spiritually.[1]

This transformative spiritual experience was steeped in Eastern philosophy, one that Stanislavski also was deeply interested in understanding. Both practitioners were interested not only in Eastern religions transformative power for the soul, but they also believed in the transformative power for their art, yet only Chekhov was able to develop this connection more deeply through his method. Stanislavski was not able, not for lack of desire but because of the political climate of the time. Dalton states:

> Anatoly Smeliansky, former Head of the Russian State Theatre School, said that he believes Chekhov carried forth spiritually what Stanislavski politically could not. Political censorship, publishing gimmicks, translation omissions, misinterpretations and teacher egos twisted these honorable intentions. What has been done in the name of truth has been a deep travesty of giant proportions.[2]

Soon after leaving the Moscow Art Theatre, Chekhov began refining his own method, which many of his contemporaries criticized as saturated with 'mysticism.' This continued interest of Chekhov's, born from his deep regard for Eastern religious practice and philosophy, was a bit too radical for many traditional Western theatre artists. The ideas that Chekhov began to espouse about the subtle (read spiritual) body and the way energy could be shared with an audience required artists with open minds and a political atmosphere of free thought, and many innovative artists embraced this exciting new technique. His technique was so widely embraced, in fact, that beginning as early as the 1920s he was able to open training programs and schools in Germany, Lithuania and England. In 1938, as developments in Europe were beginning to progress toward war (and away from free thought), Chekhov moved his school to Connecticut. Once in America he began competing with Stanislavski's other protégés—Lee Strasberg, Stella Adler, Sanford Meisner and Uta Hagen, who each had taken something different away from Stanislavski.

During the late 1940s and early 1950s, Chekhov began acting more and more in film and received an Oscar nomination for his work in *Spellbound* in 1945. After the nomination, he began coaching film actors, to which the Chekhov Technique was well suited because of the method's unique tools, which offered the distillation and concentration of character objectives through physicality, and could be tailored to any medium—be it an amphitheater or close-up frame of a film. Film actors who studied with Chekhov included Marilyn Monroe, Clint Eastwood, Anthony Quinn, Yul Brynner, Paula Strasberg, Elia Kazan, Jack Palance, Lloyd Bridges, Mala Powers and many more.

Why Are Michael Chekhov Exercises a Good Fit When Preparing Performances in Non-Traditional Spaces?

When I first begin a rehearsal process in which I am using the Michael Chekhov Technique, I often tell my favorite GPS story in order to better explain why it is worth spending an entire week(!) of rehearsal teaching this approach to the cast. The full story actually begins way before the time of my GPS, when I was training to be a director at Northwestern University. At that time, the curriculum was concentrated on the intellectual understanding of the craft, which I sorely needed. I came out of an excellent generalist theatre program at a wonderful liberal arts undergrad (Kalamazoo College) and after three years acting and directing postgraduation in New York city, I knew I wanted more focused attention on my directing approach and methodology. Northwestern provided that for me, sometimes painfully but all encompassing nonetheless. What I found was missing in my graduate work (despite the excellent education at NWU) was a bridge. I needed a bridge between my intellectual understanding of what was thematically happening in a play and the ways in which I could help my actors to physicalize those thematic ideas.

The metaphors were clear! But how to get them from the head to the body. It was the classic moment when the actor turns to the director and says, 'I know what I want it to look like but I just can't get my body to do that' or when the director turns to the actors and says, 'I know you think you are showing me the inner life of your character, but it just isn't reading.' I had often felt this frustration as an actor and now butting up against the same wall as a director was downright frustrating. If only there was some sort of shorthand/common vocabulary in which we could fast forward the organic process more physically, viscerally and effectually!

Jump forward almost a decade to when I was teaching undergraduate theatre and I decided to take my first Michael Chekhov summer workshop with the National Michael Chekhov Association. The course was thrilling! In learning the tools created by the master actor and teacher Michael Chekhov, I found a hugely effective means for building a bridge between the physicality an actor created onstage and the deep metaphors we were creating as an artistic team.

Mala Powers as a young actress when she was working with Michael Chekhov.
Credit: National Michael Chekhov Association

Mala Powers during her time teaching with the National Michael Chekhov Association.
Credit: National Michael Chekhov Association

My teachers Mala Powers, Lisa Dalton and Wil Kilroy called these exercises 'Psycho Physical Tools,' which although was somewhat intimidating at first, made sense once I began working with them. They connected the inner life to the outward effort in remarkable ways. But more than that, the exercises actually worked their magic backwards, or at least backwards from the way I was taught. This is where we get to the GPS.

Fast forward another four or five years and I am at my first MICHA (The Michael Chekhov Association, different from NMCA) International Workshop and Festival. It is another exciting amalgam of ideas and workshops. The festival is being held in Rutgers, NJ and I am staying with my cousin in Plainsboro, NJ. Being new to New Jersey, but needing to drive to the conference every morning, I relied on my now primitive GPS to get me there. There was no saving of routes or places on this device, but we thought it was mighty advanced all the same. Despite its general amazingness, it had one flaw. Every morning, during the crazy rush hour traffic, it would direct me to the highway in order to get me quickly to my destination. I knew from the unfortunate first day that the massive traffic prevented me getting to my destination in a timely manner, so the highway as a choice was out! Yet I also knew there was some great back roads ways of getting there, if only I knew how to find them (apparently, I was too busy to actually look at a map—we will skip that blip in logic if you please).

One day it occurred to me to begin driving sort of blindly in the general direction of the campus using the back roads. Lo and behold, if I held out, eventually the GPS would give up on the highway and click into the back roads way to the campus. Success! But every morning was the same (since my lack of memory when it came to general directions held out), I would continue to drive blindly in the direction of the campus and if I had faith and ignored the GPS constantly trying to send me back to the highway, it would eventually give up and get me to campus the back way. The ride was *always* faster than taking the highway. This, I explain to my cast, is the idea behind the Chekhov Technique.

Imagine that your intellect, your brain, is the highway. If you had nothing else going on in your life, the easiest fastest way to the character is to intellectually find the objective, obstacles, tactics, etc. But our lives are seldom free from traffic; we all have so much going on!

Students have tests, papers. Actors have auditions, day jobs, family—suddenly our ideas get clogged up stuck in a jam for miles and miles. Even if we magically had all the time needed to focus on the show, we would still have other roadblocks; past experiences, upbringing, internal (and therefore invisible) biases on the play and characters, etc. The intellect is no longer the fastest or easiest way to the destination of my fully realized character.

For me, the Michael Chekhov Technique is the back roads. These exercises are weird. Unclear. They make you feel a little childish and ridiculous sometimes. But keep working the tools and have faith and all the sudden one day, bam! Everything makes sense and you have 'found' the character, in rich physical detail! Most of us started our journey in acting and directing on the 'highway,' which at different times in our lives (or different shows, or different roles) has no traffic. This is all well and good until you come to the production that doesn't make sense to you, or maybe the role that eludes you. The one in which your initial ideas don't provide you with enough information or inspiration to do the job. The one you just can't get into your body. Or the one that keeps turning out the same as your last role. Or maybe the one that seems too close to you. That's when you need the Chekhov Technique.

Chekhov said, "Inspiration cannot be commanded, it is capricious. That is why the actor must always have a strong technique to fall back on."[3] The Chekhov Technique coaxes inspiration forward by allowing the imagination of the actors to lead the process of physical exploration. For me, this has proven so much more successful than relying on the intellect of the actor (or director), which so often paralyzes actors rather than freeing them. So many young actors, particularly millennials (although we all prone to it, no matter what age,) live in and through their intellect. Of course they are intelligent, but the inspiration they seek is not a finite answer to a cognitive problem, but a new way of exploring that mines the knowledge of the whole self rather than just the mind. The Chekhov Technique mines the body memory, the sensations of experiences, somatic awareness, discovery of images and impressions from the side of the brain where dreams are generated and the potential for a true collective unconscious.

I tell my cast, by all means take the highway if you like. But we are also going to work on taking these back roads. Chances are you will find as I did, the back roads get you there much faster. So the week 'wasted' not working on the play is two weeks saved finding the character and using a common vocabulary and shorthand to realize our production way before opening night. Chekhov called this an 'economy of time':

> Sometimes a period of training is mistaken in our profession for a loss of time, when we have to produce plays in four weeks. We think that if training takes years there must be something wrong . . . But when it is accomplished, it is such an economy of time. When you can laugh, cry, sing, be happy at once—when you have trained your imagination so that you can see the whole of Othello at once—that is a real economy of time.[4]

Being able to find a richly detailed portrayal of character is great for theatre *or* film. But finding character is just the beginning.

The Chekhov Technique is about energetic performance. *Non-traditional staging and performance* is about conductivity; it is a form that channels energy from actor to individual audience member and back. When you are in the audience of a non-traditional production, sometimes you see more than the actors, you also see audience—all around you. Like a moment around a campfire, the thing that attracts your attention is in the center, and yet, the experience we are all having together becomes much more tangible. I can see when someone is affected across from me. It heightens what's happening onstage. However, that can work both ways. If someone is bored across from me I can see that too. And that colors my experience. Actors must work not only to engage the audience in the story but also to conduct energy across the stage as well as across and into the audience on all sides. When the work is very strong, the energy of the audience is channeled also, right up and onto the stage, and then across the room. In non-traditional staging and performance (NTS&P) work, we both send a performance out into the audience and pull an audience into our experience. Yet unlike the pull of film or TV, it is not a solitary pull, it is a communal pull.

In the nickelodeon TV series *Avatar: The Last Airbender* there is a character named 'Zuko' who is able to send fire out of his body. His evil sister can also send fire, but her specialty is electricity. Although Zuko cannot send electricity like his sister can, his uncle teaches him how to channel electricity through his body. He then becomes able to catch her energy, direct it around his heart and through his body and then redirect away from him. In NTS&P we all have the ability to redirect energy. It begins on the stage but once it is sent out, the energy can shoot through the audience in any direction and then often jumps back onstage altering the performance. It is the quintessence of live performance. It is the observer effect, but the audience as well as actors are the ones observed. We are all changed by the experience.

Who Is This Book For?

Late in his career, Chekhov wrote his seminal text *To the Actor: On the Technique of Acting*. The book describes in detail his technique as well as detailed descriptions of his exercises. This book, as well as many others he had written in his time, are incredible resources and amazing insights into imaginative physical performance.

They can be, however, a bit intimidating at first. When I first taught acting at the undergraduate level, I was very interested and excited by all I had read about and by Michael Chekhov, but was unsure of how to incorporate his exercises into the lesson plans for my Acting 1 undergraduate course in a way that was accessible to both my students and myself as a novice teacher. I was also having the same issues with my productions, I wanted to thread some of the ideas and exercises into my rehearsal, but wasn't sure how. I had not yet attended a workshop, conference or festival but I still valued the work!

So many of us who work in academia struggle with how to craft a course, a syllabus, a lesson or rehearsal plan based on our prior education that may or may not match the program in which we are employed. Many acting teachers in small liberal arts programs hold directing MFAs, which are a must if you will be directing within the season but may not have adequately prepared you to teach acting. Sometimes acting teachers hold BFAs and MFAs from conservatories, which train a very different kind of student than the traditional BA student, and yet faculties are often asked to make the leap with little guidance. And as most of us generally train to practice, teaching performance is often a DIY endeavor in and of itself. Finding the right resources to help craft the strongest courses for your students are at a premium. Finding resources to train undergraduate actors during the rehearsal process are pure gold. I wrote this book to be the book

I needed in my first few years of teaching and directing at the under-graduate level. The one that bridges the extremely exciting ideas of Michael Chekhov to the needs of the modern-day university, college or performing arts high school.

This book is also a way for Michael Chekhov enthusiasts to mix-up their lesson/rehearsal plans and incorporate some new takes on some well-worn ideas. No longer a novice to the field, I know I appreciate when new resources arrive that can give me fresh ways to connect to the work and engage my students. Oftentimes it's like a great ATHE (Association for Theatre in Higher Education) workshop or MICHA festival or NMCA 'Deeper by Design' session, you come away feeling excited to incorporate the new ideas that complement or expand on what you are already doing in fun new ways. My hope is that, no matter where you are in your career, this book can be a wonderful new resource for you.

In addition to some new takes on traditional Chekhovian Technique, this book also has the added gift of some excellent additional exercises from master teachers Wil Kilroy, co-founder of the National Michael Chekhov Association, and Samantha Norton, classically trained opera and vocal coach/fight choreographer. Wil Kilroy has contributed many wonderful improvisational exercises and Samantha Norton adds Chekhovian-inspired physical/vocal technique into the mix. Both of these brilliant contributors offer even more exercises to try in your production and/or class. In addition, at the end of each chapter will be an essay from an outside expert with specific advice on non-traditional staging for those who might already have an upcoming production in the works. Enjoy advice on staging and production from:

- *Lynn Musgrave:* A director entering her fourth decade staging in the round at Theatre in the Round's arena (Minneapolis) along with other thrust and smaller arenas in the upper Midwest.
- *Ed Menta:* A director who has primarily worked on the thrust stage at Kalamazoo College for over 30 years.
- *Karel Blakeley:* A set designer who has worked in the round, thrust and proscenium in a black box theatre at Le Moyne College for over 30 years.
- *Heath Hansum:* A lighting designer who has worked in the round, thrust, alley and proscenium at Bucknell University, Bloomsburg Theatre and the Theatre at Breadloaf, at Middlebury College.

- *Susan Picinich:* A costume designer in universities and regional theatres who works in all kinds of venues including in the round.
- *Lisa Dalton:* An actor, director and teacher, who, academically and professionally, has incorporated the Michael Chekhov Technique into multiple staging forms for more than 35 years.

Although much of this book focuses on the subject of *non-traditionally staged productions* (in the round, thrust, alley and site specific), the majority of it focuses on the subject of *non-traditional performance technique.* This technique can be utilized and/or adapted for any kind of production, film and/or acting course where a more visceral connection to the audience is the goal. The Michael Chekhov Technique is beautifully rich and powerful method for *non-traditional performance* and these newly imagined exercises offer playful new doorways into this important and transformational work.

P.S. This book is also for you, actors and directors—student actors and directors, faculty actors and directors, professional actors and directors. As a resource for exercises specific to a more visceral kind of performance, Michael Chekhov is your guy. This book is an entry point and/or a way to add more tools about the Chekhov Technique to your toolbox. More tricks to your magic act. More veggies for your garden. More mermaids in your ocean. Are these enough metaphors for you? Good. Then jump onboard the train (last one) and get started.

Notes

1 Lisa Dalton, *Murder of Talent: How Pop Culture Is Killing "IT."* forthcoming, 2017.
2 Lisa Dalton, *Murder of Talent: How Pop Culture Is Killing "IT."* forthcoming, 2017.
3 Michael Chekhov, *To the Actor: On the Technique of Acting.* London: Routledge, 2002, p. xxxvii.
4 Michael Chekhov, *Lessons for the Professional Actor,* edited by Deirdre Hurst Du Prey. New York: Performing Arts Publications, 1985, p. 33.

Radium Girls by D.W. Gregory. In the round production directed by Anjalee Deshpande Hutchinson, lighting design by Heath Hansum, costume design by Jenny Kenyon, scenic design by F. Elaine Williams. Bucknell University 2015. Credit: Mark Hutchinson

Credit: drawing courtesy of Pablo Guerra-Monje

2

HONORING THE OBLIGATION

When we choose tell a story through the medium of the theatre, we accept many obligations. We have an obligation to the playwright, to deliver his or her words and ideas as clearly and accurately as possible. We have an obligation to the audience, not to waste their time but to share engaging, entertaining and meaningful productions. As actors we have obligations to the director, to collaborate with her or him to create the most expressive, most masterfully crafted interpretations of the text as possible. We have obligations to the designers to both showcase and utilize their designs to the best of our abilities. We have obligations to the producers, the theatre companies, the subscribers, the donors, the history of theatre, those who have come before us and even the very boards themselves. If you have ever taken an inspirational acting course or been directed by an exciting director, you must have heard at least some of this before.

Similarly, when we are acting in a *non-traditional* performance, we commit deeply in our obligation to our *stage partners*. The other actors you work with rely on you in different ways because they cannot always share their intentions with the audience. If one side of the audience gets a deeply personal view of your character's transitional moment, exciting revelation or underlying subtext, you know that another side of the audience is sure to have missed it. That is the time when your partners must honor their obligation to you. They must find ways to continue telling the story through their characters, filling in the gaps with their choices, and you must do the same for them. Only in this way can the audience feel completely immersed in the play. Each actor must not only tell the story of her/his own character, but also be prepared to open his or her own awareness to the stories all the other actors are telling and find ways to support, contrast, highlight and reveal those stories as much as needed in any given moment.

Exercise 2.1 Free Play/Open Swim

Inspired by MC's Ideas on Ensemble Work

Many children of the 1970s and 1980s in the US may remember the time after swim lessons but before getting picked up by your parents known as 'Open Swim.' It was a time to just be in the water with your friends and not worry about having to work hard getting the breast stroke right or learning how to dive properly. You were in the water, had warmed up by this point and were given permission to just goof around. You let whatever 'showed up' in that moment guide the play. Maybe you felt the need to twirl around or fish tail in the shallow end, which led to a game of mermaids or sharks. Maybe you were inspired to slap your arms against the water making huge sounds, which turned out to be hilariously funny to your friend who then joined in. Maybe you just let yourself sink to the bottom and imagined being dead.

It didn't matter, because nothing was really off-limits. You could be by yourself or be with others. You were inspired in the moment and nothing was premeditated. You were free. Much of the play when we are children (or at least when I was a kid) was this same sort of 'open swim' idea, whether in the water or on land. As performers, this awareness of the world immediately around us, awareness of inspiration found in the moment and often with each other, is vital. Believe it or not, building the ability to allow for a spontaneous kinesthetic response to this kind of stimuli is the key to deeply committed and engaged performances shared between partners and among ensembles. This exercise, especially over time, will begin to rebuild those free play muscles that you at one time probably had zero problems accessing.

In his *To the Actor: On the Technique of Acting*, Chekhov speaks on the importance of ensemble work: "Only artists united by true sympathy into an improvising ensemble can know the joy of unselfish, common creation."[1] Chekhov invests in the idea that all theatre in its highest incarnation is collaborative, and that investing in collaborative improvisation paradoxically builds the actor's abilities to fully express their individuality. They build this ability to express by trusting in the group, which in turn allows them a kind of freedom unparalleled in other activities of life: "A new and gratifying sensation of complete confidence in yourself, along with the sensation of freedom and inner richness, will be the reward for all of your efforts."[2]

In this exercise, we allow the actor's individuality to find its expression through improvisation with the group. This group work allows the actor to build the trust necessary to take deep risks through a constant process of give and take with her/his partners. Chekhov says of this kind of work: "An improvising ensemble lives in a constant process of giving and taking. A small hint from a partner—a glance, a pause, a new unexpected intonation, a movement, a sigh or even a barely perceptible change of tempo can become a creative impulse and invitation to the other."[3] Here we invite the actors to play:

Coaching Free Play/Open Swim

Based on Chekhov's Ideas on Ensemble Work ('Making Friends' with the Space and Each Other)

Objective: To warm up actors physically and vocally as well as warm up their ability to connect and respond kinesthetically to the other actors in the ensemble, the space and the play.

Coach:

- Begin this exercise with a short meditation (see Exercise 5.1 or 5.2 in Chapter 5 if you need an idea but any relaxation/meditation/ mindful breathing exercise can work here) or a few minutes of no talking. Having your actors lie on the ground, slowing their breath, relaxing each individual body part and then their whole body is one way to achieve this. Once your ensemble is very relaxed and/or in a meditative state, bring them slowly out of their introspection by asking them to look for the urge to move.

(continued)

(continued)

Actors beginning 'Free Play/Open Swim'.
Credit: Gordon Wenzel

Coach:

- Ask yourself what wants to move?
- What would feel good?
- What needs a stretch?
- Now follow that urge, and slowly, allowing your eyes to open with a soft focus or gaze, let your body explore the movement. Stay focused on your own experience right now, avoid direct eye contact or connection to others at this point, just keep everyone who isn't in your body in soft peripheral focus.

As they begin to move, continue coaching:

- Ask yourself what would feel fun to move, what part of your body wants to jiggle or bop or shimmy or slosh around. Follow that movement. Play with it. Repeat it over and over until it feels right.
- Can you make the movement bigger? More expansive? Can you make it a whole body movement?
- Can you make it smaller? Contracting? A whole body contraction?
- Don't get stuck on just one movement, keep exploring. Try different tempos and vary the pace!
- As soon as you get bored, move on to something new. What else would feel fun to do? What has 'shown up' here today? Feel free to explore new levels, move around the space, check out the space we are in and play with it.

- Maybe you have an image? Of an animal or a machine or the way the light moves and you want to play with it—let yourself explore! If you find something you like doing, repeat it, make it more expansive. When you are ready give it breath! Give it sound! No words yet but begin to play with sound. Your voice is an extension of your body!

After a short period working with their own bodies and then the space around them (give them a gentle coaching hint to do so if they didn't already), begin to move the actors into working with each other. If they start to do this before they have had sufficient time on their own, gently guide them back (this is important—don't skip the private time!).

Continue coaching:

- When you are ready, begin noticing the other people in the space with you. You don't have to connect right away, just allow the awareness of others in the space to slowly permeate your experience. Is anyone doing anything fun you'd like to join in on? Would you like to try to do what they are doing? Notice.
- When you are ready, try beginning to allow yourself to act on something someone else is doing—whether they are close to you or far away. You can repeat someone's actions to try them on or join them. Or maybe you do something that contrasts what they are doing—do they like it? Does it become a part of the game? What happens? When you are ready, begin to let noticing other people grow into playing with other people.

Once you have gotten this far, the ensemble will begin to take it from there. All of a sudden, ridiculous, poignant, crazy little mini plays will begin to emerge. The only coaching I tend to do after this point is occasionally to say 'Don't get stuck' to those playing the same game for too long (you'll know). Sometimes I push players to try different tempos—if they aren't out of breath or running around at least once during the exercise, they aren't fully committing. Sometimes I urge them to 'connect with others' for those who feel particularly solitary.

Actors engaged in 'Free Play/Open Swim'.
Credit: Gordon Wenzel

Actors engaged in 'Free Play/Open Swim'.
Credit: Gordon Wenzel

If an actor does not feel like connecting after a prompt, I leave him or her alone for that day. More than one day of that will require a discussion outside of rehearsal, which generally includes: 'It's great that you are finding inspiration within yourself and the space around you but I need you to also allow connections to the people in the ensemble, a vital component of this work is connection.'

After 15–30 minutes of this, I ask them to find a place to end or a place of stillness and rest. Once that is over, we do a quick reflection as a group on what was most fun or resonated with them the most in the exercise. I also allow them to 'pass' if they would rather not comment at this time. During this discussion, shared connections emerge, are remembered and deepen the ensemble's bond. The group is warmed

Actors engaged in 'Free Play/Open Swim'.
Credit: Gordon Wenzel

up physically and somewhat vocally as well. They are ready to work on text or blocking or the next item of production/course business. I find this a vastly more useful way of warming up than your basic stretches in a circle. Mainly because it also 'warms up' the ability to connect to one's inner impulses as well as connect to each other in kinesthetic, unfiltered and unpremeditated ways.

But the real magic of this exercise is if you faithfully incorporate it into your rehearsal process. Each time you work this exercise, you will notice less and less need for coaching. Helping them begin and then a few 'don't get stucks' along the way usually suffices. Some ensembles don't need any coaching at all. Incorporate the exercise into the whole first week every day if possible before you begin rehearsal each night. Then at least once a week for the next several weeks of rehearsal. Then once you begin doing runs every night, bring the exercise back nightly. Even devoting 10–15 minutes of time to this exercise will not only reconnect your actors to each other in a palpable way, but also themes from the story you are telling will inevitably emerge.

Are you doing a tragedy? Death will show up in the free play—often comically, occasionally with zombies. Is there a romance? Men and women will team up against each other in some game that surfaces. Or start clown flirting. Or switch sexes. Animals that represent characters will bubble to the top. Alliances will be forged, enemies will be confronted, great battles will be won and lost—but all without the pressure to 'perform' toward a specific premeditated goal. All playful. Somehow this exercise allows the actors to 'play' with the topic on an almost subconscious level, without premeditating a thing. And playing with the themes before they take on the text and the full immersion into their characters allows for them to connect more deeply to the material.

Impressive what a little Open Swim can do for your deep dive into the world of the play.

When used throughout the rehearsal process (I like using it weekly until the production week and then I employ the tool nightly), the process goes through many transformations but always yields new impulses, new connections and new avenues of exploration. If you want, you may also encourage the actors (after already having spent a good deal time with no specific prompts on the production) to invite their character into the free play, however it is that they may 'show up.' Encourage the them not to premeditate but to allow for discovery. Inform the actors that the characters may show up at any age (before the event of the play, after) or in any mood or even as a dream of what the character could be. When encouraged to invite characters in, sometimes moments not lived in the play could show up to give satisfaction or warning to impulses not met in the action of the play.

Be sure to start these and all exercises where actors engage each other with a strict rule 'to take care of yourself, take care of your space and take care of each other.' This rule (handed down from legendary theatre sage Bill Morris of Le Moyne College) should be further explained to maintain the boundaries of safety on the stage, safety with their own bodies in the space and the respectful explorations of impulses especially when they engage the physical bodies of others. This is particularly important if you 'invite' characters into play. Discuss what respectful exploration means. This for me often means having the cast agree to what's okay (e.g., we can touch each other) and what's not okay (no butt, genitals, breasts, mouth—etc.). Give each person a chance to differ from the group—'I don't want to be touched today at all' or 'nobody touch my legs today' or 'I am okay if you touch my lips'—etc. Each cast will be different. Some cast may want there to be no rules. I encourage you to ask them to find at least one boundary line, otherwise—in an effort to please either the director or each other—they may offer too much and silence their desire to be safe rather than to honor their needs. Some actors may argue that spontaneity is lost by establishing rules. I completely disagree with this. Structure can allow for far more freedom to make creative, rather than easy choices. Your impulses will find creative solutions for their outlet rather than the first 'easy' idea. A character wanting to kiss another character and not being able to might result in some beautiful abstract movements or silly free play or even another interpretation of what a kiss can be. Actors should trust their imaginations to 'fill in.'

For further information on creating safe spaces when exploring physicality, I highly recommend reading 'Sex & violence: Practical approaches for dealing with extreme stage physicality' by Adam Noble which was featured in the magazine *Fight Master* in May 2011 (a pdf of this article is available on the companion website to this book). I have used the ideas Noble presents with actors and directors in all of my classes and productions since 2012 with strong results. The clear guidelines offer assessable ways to establish safe space while still offering the foundations of creative exploration. These guidelines inspired the methodology detailed in the paragraph above, which keeps Free Play safe as well as exciting and fun.

Exercise 2.2 The 'Here' Silent Story
Based on MC's Tools Radiating and Receiving

When you are about half of the way through your process and/or your class, this is a good time to return to the idea of Honoring the Obligation and try the 'Here' exercise. This exercise activates a deeper understanding and sensitivity in your actors to the needs of the audience. In the beginning stages of rehearsal, actors are often preoccupied with creating characters and justifying movement, which can be especially tricky in the sometimes constant motion that is non-traditional staging. In the round, actors can never spend too long in one place for fear of losing the audience with whom you are sharing only your back. When done well, this can look more natural and less 'stagey' because you are never actually 'cheating out' to anyone. When done poorly it looks like you are dancing around the stage for no apparent reason.

In-the-Round/Thrust Staging

Tip 1: When acting in the round, try to stand just off from one another. So if I am supposed to be speaking to your face, my right shoulder will be across from your right shoulder and my right eye will be in line with your right eye.

> *Tip 2*: Whenever possible, find the vomitorium passage (vom)/
> entrance/exit point and find ways to turn your back to that
> vom. The closer you are to the vom point, the more of the
> audience that will be able to see you.
>
> *Tip 3*: Angles are your friends! Play to the audience but also
> work those diagonals, especially those with and exit/entrance
> point.

Justifying movement becomes essential to the feel and flow of the piece. Part of this justification is the meaningful connections to the other characters. So much time is often spent creating these connections early on in NTS productions. However, connecting to an audience is just as important as connecting to your partners and can make or break the strength of how an audience *perceives* your movement. Justifying an action physically ('I am thirsty, I need a glass of water') vs. justifying the action psychologically ('What he just said makes me feel embarrassed and my face feels hot and flushed. I need a glass of water') can make a huge difference in the meaningful connections the audience makes to your character. If we focus on our connections with other characters (the responses we want from them) more deeply than our connection with the audience (revealing what our character is going through), we threaten to lose audience interest. In an effort to pursue one goal, one relationship, we can lose the other. The audience is the other partner in the space. In a traditional rehearsal process on a proscenium stage, an awareness of the audience usually comes in the week after tech but before performance, with continued notes on turning out and sharing with the audience what you have discovered, as an actor and as an ensemble. Although this is not ideal even on the proscenium, the audience is often treated as the 'lesser' partner to be dealt with at the end of rehearsal.

In NTS&P productions, one must consider this audience component differently. Finding ways to tell the story, not just to one but also to many audiences, has to become part of the process of creation itself. What you create by yourself and with partners must always intentionally seek to reveal what each individual audience side needs and wants to see. The following exercise heightens an ensemble's awareness of what these audience needs are, and how to incorporate them into the natural flow of movement within the play.

Chekhov often refers to the audience actor dynamic as integral to the process of engaged theatre making. He refers to this phenomenon as something that is in the actor's control through the terms Radiating and Receiving. *"To radiate onstage means to give, to send out. Its counterpart is to receive. True acting is a constant change of the two."*[4] In this exercise, we utilize the ensemble to assist individual actors' ability to radiate and receive from the audience, an integral component of NTS&P.

Coaching The 'Here' Silent Story

Based on Chekhov's Tools Radiating and Receiving

Objective: To raise actor awareness to audiences on every side and practice sharing and inviting every audience side into the play.

Coach:

- Begin this exercise by asking your actors to think about their movements and blocking throughout the play. If you are early in the process, they can improv this physical score. Tell them they will be working on a variation of 'The Silent Story' directing exercise some of them may have encountered in the past.
- Can you do an entire scene without words—just movement?
- Can the audience still tell what is going on?
- Does the movement justify the transitions and interactions between the characters?
- Tell them they will be doing an entire silent or paraphrased run. Choose which is right for your production.
- Now ask one portion of the cast to sit on each side of the audience. If you are working in the round, one-fourth of your actors should be seated on any one side. None of the actors should sit together even if they are on the same side. They should all try sitting in various seats (or standing positions) away from each other. Ask your stage managers, assistant stage managers and anyone else in the room to join. You should too.

(continued)

(*continued*)

Coach:

- When actors perform a scene, they should get up from the audience to perform, sitting back in the audience in a new seat when the next set of actors jump up to perform their scene.
- Invite yourself to the party. Everyone in the audience should yell 'Here' whenever they don't have a clear view of anyone's face who is performing in the scene. Imagine that the performers are pulling you in; help them by giving your full attention and asking to be pulled in whenever you start losing the connection.
- When actors hear the word 'Here' from any direction while they performing, they have three jobs to do:

  1. Shift their body slightly, or to a new angle, so they share their face with more of the audience. Tell them to 'feel it out,' if their partner shifts their body slightly, they might not have to! But they must be constantly in connection/silent communication with their partners in order to share the story. Coach them to work together with their partner/s to physically open the scene to the most amount of people.
  2. Coach actors to project their intentions with their whole body, not just their face—tell actors to 'emote with your back as if you can send out what is on your face through your back into the audience.' The actual physicality of this can be large or subtle depending on the style of the piece and/or the moment in the play. Coach actors to keep their focus on sending their character's intention energetically strong no matter what the style or moment. You'll be surprised how much you can communicate when focusing your energies on sharing in all directions.
  3. Share with the actors that if a partner cannot turn toward the person in the audience who is yelling/speaking/communicating during a major beat within the scene, it is the obligation of the partner who can move to share the moment with the audience who cannot see their partner's face. That means their response is as important (if not more sometimes) as what they are expressing—and vice versa.

If you are halfway through your rehearsal process, hopefully the blocking (or general patterns of movement) will be second nature to the actors. If not, it is still a useful exercise to improv the movement; if actors don't remember the blocking or are worried about confusing the blocking, encourage them to think beyond the 'final result' and to focus instead on the energy and intent of the scene in order to make new discoveries. The exact blocking can always return as the focus later. The overall goal of the cast will be to make the physicality justified and meaningful, but the added impact of having their audience ask them to share more vocally and physically will shift their attention toward sharing more broadly. This asking will force the actors out of their comfort zone of performing for each other (and the director/instructor) into the intentionality of performing to, for and with an audience. Sometimes this exercise is all it takes for the ensemble to make connections and big leaps into stronger more viscerally connected work. The kind of work your audience can palpably feel.

Exercise 2.3 Sculpting in Space: Back, Front and Side

Based on MC's Ideas on Qualities of Movement—Sculpting/Molding

In many of Chekhov's texts, he refers to the Qualities of Movement exercises as ways to access physicality that can easily translate onto the stage: "This [These] exercises will constantly enable you to create forms for whatever you do on the stage."[5] In this version of the exercise, Wil Kilroy focuses on this translatable physicality from all vantage points, concentrating on every part of the body as a vital tool for expression.

Coaching Sculpting in Space

Based on Chekhov's Tools Qualities of Movement—Sculpting/Molding

By Wil Kilroy

Objective: Allow actors to increase their kinesthetic awareness 360 degrees around them, as well as grow an awareness of gesturing with the full body in all directions.

(continued)

(continued)

Coach:

- All actors are instructed to distribute themselves in the space, facing all angles, and putting the focus on themselves for the moment and not the rest of the ensemble.
- Instructions are then given to begin 'sculpting' the space around them as if it were clay. Beginning at first with just a hand, being sure to utilize the imagination to feel resistance, just as a sculptor might feel as they work with clay.
- In Michael Chekhov's acting technique this is referred to as 'molding,' and the substance corresponds to the element of earth. Once the actors are successfully working with their hands, instruction is given to proceed with the rest of the body joining into this sculpting process. Now the arm begins to carve through the space, and now the torso, and now a step is taken.

Actors engaged in 'Sculpting' exercise.
Credit: Gordon Wenzel

- Particular care needs to be taken when beginning to walk as the rising of the heel must be sculpted with resistance, as well as the lift of the foot into the air and the subsequent touching of the ball of the foot back to the earth.
- If the pace seems to quicken, and the imaginary 'clay' begins to be ignored, call out an element change to the image of working with 'stone.' The actors must now imagine carving through stone with every part of their body. This will increase focus and reduce the tempo so that the actor can have awareness of each and every body part—a necessity to any stellar performance.
- To stimulate the imagination, continue to call out other element changes such as dirt, or plaster, or cornmeal.
- In order to practice for theatre in the round, actors are encouraged to sculpt in all directions and all levels, thus they are not focusing their actions to any one direction but instead work within the full circumference of their space.
- Actors are also coached to "sculpt behind you, above you, below you, to each side of you." This will again extend their awareness beyond the typical forward focus used on a proscenium stage, but also add endless creativity to their eventual gestures onstage.
- Once the physical sculpting is successful, the actors are coached to add voice. This might be simply counting, or reciting the alphabet, or lines of text that they have memorized. This allows them to also sculpt with their voice and develop the important body/voice connection, which can lead to character creation.
- After the actors have spent time on their own sculpting, it's time to bring them into improvisation. Actors now sculpt with their bodies and voices toward each other, and communicate via their movement and sound, being sure to fully 'listen' and then to respond.
- Actors continue to be coached to sculpt in all directions, even when responding, which might cause them to turn their backs and sculpt in a new direction. These changes of direction will allow actors to continue being comfortable performing in all directions as required by theatre in the round.

Exercise 2.4 Voice Shapes: Playing
with Archetypal Voices

Based on MC's Tools Archetype, Tempo and
Qualities of Movement

Gesture has always been an important part of Chekhov's theory and technique. When referring in specific to the tool 'Archetypal Gesture', Chekhov defines this kind of gesture as, "One which serves as an original model for all possible gestures of the same kind."[6] Connected to Carl Jung's ideas that there are universal, mythic characters that reside in the psyches of people across all cultures of the world, Chekhov further defines these ideas through physicality, with the premise that there are universal gestures that are common between all peoples within the world. In the exercise here, Samantha Norton further develops Chekhov's premise in order to explore vocal gestures as the natural extensions of the physicality work we began with Qualities of Movement. In addition, she introduces the idea of using tempo.

Coaching Voice Shapes

Based on Chekhov's Ideas of Archetype, Tempo and
Qualities of Movement

By Samantha Norton

Welcome to the world of Chekhov's qualities of movement translated to the voice. Our voices are capable of creating a plethora of archetypal characters using some of Chekhov's techniques. Voice shaping can be applied to any of Chekhov's techniques.

Objective: To add dimension and depth to vocal character choices.

Coach:

- To begin, ask your students if they can 'impersonate' or allow themselves to embrace the stereotype of the following archetypal characters through the physicality as well as the voice. The numbers 1–10 can be used or even gibberish if an actor is nervous about improvising with words. For this exercise we use the word 'stereotype' to embrace all the information you know

---

about a type of character from what is culturally accepted as the way this kind of person talks, moves, behaves. It is only a starting point so there is no need to be afraid of embracing a physical and vocal exploration.

- Tell your actors to also beware of adding a quality! This is not necessarily a mean or nice football coach—it is the essential football coach in all of our collective imaginations. In addition, try to avoid judging the character. Do not choose to make the supermodel 'dumb' or the hero 'arrogant' because you decide to impose a quality based on your judgment of models or heroes. Embrace these characters without judgment:

Coach:

- Read this list out loud, one by one, and linger for a bit on each archetype, asking actors to explore what this person moves and sounds like. All actors should be working at the same time, paying attention to only their own work:

  - Football coach
  - Supermodel
  - Preacher
  - Auctioneer
  - President
  - Drag queen
  - Taxi cab driver
  - Librarian
  - Kindergarten teacher
  - Stand-up comedian
  - Super hero
  - Mother
  - Villain
  - Computer technician
  - Professor
  - Sportscaster

- Facilitators—feel free to add to this list! Especially if you have archetypes that resonate more deeply with your production,

(continued)

(*continued*)

characters in the production or roles characters play in relationship to one another—like mothering or being the funny guy.

Coach:

- Ask the actors if most of the sounds your students created were
  gender specific. Were they able to 'impersonate' beyond using
  high and low pitches? Discuss as a group.
- Now ask them to try some of these characters as the opposite
  sex. Take note and point out students that are beginning to add
  more qualities to the sound such as tempo and articulation.
  They are on the right track.
- Now let the students play with qualities that are the opposite of
  how they believe the character would sound. For instance, what
  if the supermodel had the voice of the football coach or the kindergarten teacher had the delivery of a stand-up comedian.
- Once they have played with that, ask them again to return to the
  archetypal voice of a character (from the list above) and then
  ask them to add qualities to those vocal choices. Have them
  walk the space and try out any characters from the previous
  list (they can stick with one or try many different ones as the
  exercises goes on) with the qualities you call out from this list:

  1. Staccato (short, sharp, fast, monotone, loud sounds, like an
      auctioneer); Legato (melodic, smooth, slow, soft sounds,
      like a supermodel).
  2. Molding (deliberate, slow, contemplative, like a professor).
  3. Flowing (melodic, frequent change in volume, like a
      preacher).
  4. Flying (very melodic, light soft sounds, like a kindergarten
      teacher).
  5. Radiating (full sounds can be fast/slow, sharp or expansive
      like a superhero or a villain).

- Once they have tried many different qualities, ask them first
  about their experiences and what surprised them. Then ask
  which archetypal voice might fit their characters and why? Is it

how they see themselves? How others see them? Perhaps they can think of new archetypal roles their characters might play, either in their own minds (I am always mothering everyone) or each other (she is such a diva).

- Then ask them what qualities they can add to give further texture and develop the voice of this person. What contrasting surprising qualities might the actors try? Give them time to work on their own and then have them return and demonstrate their discoveries one at a time to the group. Be prepared to welcome new and unique character revelations that arise through the voice! Encourage these wonderful unexpected ways into the characters.

Advice from the Pros: Using the Four Brothers for Non-Traditional Staging

By Lisa Loving Dalton

As a director, what do you do when there is no upstage or downstage, no stage right or left? These questions arise when we work with

Lisa Loving Dalton, director, actor, teacher and president of the National Michael Chekhov Association.

Credit: Lisa Loving Dalton

alternative staging patterns. These patterns can feel intimidating to the actors as well as to directors and designers. Expanded skill sets are needed. One can no longer rely upon the repertoire of foundational tools developed for proscenium styles.

Here are three distinct recommendations for directors:

1. Ask yourself and your cast leading questions for practical purposes specific to each production. Chekhov's 'Four Brothers' tools can be helpful here.
2. Build the long-term skill sets of your performers.
3. Consider brief tips on non-traditional staging specifically for director/designers.

Ask Leading Questions for Each Production

To explore the specific needs of a given production, help can come from the Chekhov Technique's tool entitled 'The Four Brothers of Art,' based on traits Chekhov believed to be present in all actors when they were engaged in a peak performance. By asking leading questions using the four brothers—the 'feelings' of Beauty, Ease, Entirety and Form—directors can better visualize and create engaging productions that utilize the unique strengths of the non-traditional stage.

The Feeling of Beauty invites us to ask: What is beautiful, unique and wonderful in this staging structure? What can we do here that we could not do in a proscenium? How can we create a stronger relationship with the audience, *here*? How can this story reveal itself in this space, unlike any other space? Can we entertain more people in a more intimate setting? Can we give a more multidimensional experience to the spectator, with entrances among their midst? Can we create more focus on the performer? Why was this performance space created this way instead of a proscenium? Imagine asking the creators of the space what their intention was. The regular audiences come here, in part, for its non-traditional structure. Knowing what about that appeals to them helps you craft the performance to ensure fulfilling the audience's desire. Find the Feeling of Beauty, and your creativity is freed from fear of the differences this form presents.

The Feeling of Ease invites us to ask is there something here that makes me uneasy? Can I find a way to see the beauty of it? Am I willing to at least pretend that this form is easy to play? What do we need to

Walk Across Egypt. Directed by Lisa Loving Dalton. Artisan Center Theater, Hurst, 2009.

Credit: Alan Smith

do to convey the images to the audience in this environment? Ease can instantly appear the moment one sees the Beauty of the form.

The Feeling of Entirety/Wholeness invites us to ask is there some aspect of this form that feels incomplete? Do I miss the feeling of the frame of the proscenium? Is there a way I can see this form as a whole in and of itself? Feelings of Beauty and Ease are often lost when 'entirety' or a sense of the whole is missing.

The Feeling of Form is clearly the fundamental question in this book. What are the physical limits and opportunities unique to this form? What is beautiful about that? Ask yourself if you are comfortable with the spectator positioned inside the walls? Inside the Fourth Wall? What happens when their feet are in the actor's way? Feelings of Beauty, Ease and Entirety are often fractured when the form (the physical shape the production takes) is judged to be ugly, incomplete, missing something or too challenging, thus causing panic.

Actively engage Chekhov's Four Brothers' tools to create an artistic frame for the entire ensemble involved. Intentionally ask: How is this the ideal form for this production? This question will lead to discoveries about the Beauty, Ease and Entirety of a production, activating a sense of enthusiasm and appreciation for this particular form. In the safety of this, creativity is fertilized.

As a director, prepare your answers to these questions. If the space is a regular performance venue, interview your producer, past directors or the person who knows this space the best, asking for advice on basic staging. Engage a feeling of ease about vulnerability and implications of inadequacy that may rear in your head. This bold inquiry develops your own confident excitement about the form. Everyone wants a good

Walk Across Egypt. Directed by Lisa Loving Dalton. Artisan Center Theater, Hurst, 2009.

Credit: Alan Smith

show and there is never a reason to waste time, energy and resources reinventing the wheel.

Then, in your earliest gathering of the cast, crew and designers, assess your ensemble's knowledge and experience level with the form of this stage. Lead them through a group experience, up on their feet, where they actively awaken, one at a time, their own sense of Beauty, Ease, Entirety and Form. Side-coach them subtly into seeing these if you sense they are not. Follow this by sharing some of the basic tried and true blocking recommendations for the form such as:

- The power of playing the diagonals.
- Center, away from audience, as upstage, closer to audience as downstage.
- Corners and goal posts as mini-proscenia.

Rotate the cast sitting them in different sections of the audience so they can experience the staging from the spectator's point of view. This ensures that everyone involved understands the unique opportunities and means of exploiting this stage structure. It allows the entire ensemble to engage in creative problem solving.

Building Long-Term Performance Skills

Three primary performance's skills necessary for non-traditional staging are:

1. Developing 360 degrees of sensibility, sensitivity or awareness.

2. Mastering the art of movement that maintains audience connection.
3. Mastering the form's unique opportunities.

The 360-Degree Artist can convey images through any part of the body: front, side, back, top, middle, or bottom. An audience can be looking at the feet, the profile or the back of the head and shoulders and still be clear on what is happening in this moment of the character's life. All training in Michael Chekhov's approach will awaken a sense of the space in relation to the body. This training ideally cultivates full-bodied response that includes a particular training of the awareness of backspace and side-space.

Actors must build fluidity of expanding and contracting in all body parts, most notably the spinal area between chest and scapula as these parts can convey much to audiences on all sides. The thoracic area of the spine frames the heart and is the area Chekhov referred to as 'The Ideal Artistic Center' (IAC) in the chest. Chekhov describes this IAC as about three inches below the collarbone intersection, and about three inches inside. It is the point in the human being that seems to house the sense of self one points to when you declare "This is me, mine, or I am." It is where most people point when responding to a statement with the question "Who me?"

Many people mistake this as an area of immobility. This "IAC" area, ideally, is supported by a posteriorly curved segment of the spine with our ribs attached. These bone structures envelop the lungs and diaphragm that influence our tone and breath. The quality of our sound is considered to be 37 percent of our communication. When this area's true potential for mobility remains undeveloped, artists deny their most heartfelt expression.

The muscle-bound athlete rarely can allow any movement in this segment of the spine. It seemingly is permanently thrusting forward, with the shoulders hoisted back, ribs protruding beyond the breastbone. Thus, it can lead to spinal stress, causing an anterior curve pressing forward instead of the natural thoracic curve toward the back. Military spine, with cervical straightening, often occurs, radiating inflexibility of character with strong will.

The psychological effect of chest immobility on the audience is one of impermeability, invincibility. Viewed from any perspective, the actor bound in this way seems unaffected emotionally. Most of these actors rely upon voice, hand gestures and facial expression to convey emotion. If one limits the audience's ability to see the hands or face, communication suffers greatly. Impulse from the lower parts the body or in the limbs can be more prominently displayed in the front of the body. This is often an undesirable limitation of communication for the audience of NTS.

For the performer with an extreme posterior curvature, the head frequently protrudes, causing neck strain and caving of the shoulders. The curve is hyper-extended toward the back. The shoulders counter, falling forward. The pelvis tucks under and no impulses from the will centers are able to rise up. Two impressions dominate.

The shy person generally withholds their IAC, such that the spine cannot present itself upright in this segment. A sense of low self-esteem is conveyed from all but the frontal view where, from the face and sometimes the hands, we can see the body language of other feelings and will impulses. Woe to the audience segment that can't see the face.

This position can alternatively generate a perception of 'headiness,' with complete lack of connection to physical action and emotion. Images appear 'nerdy,' logical, and might express in the sagittal plane primarily. The appearance is, from most angles, that the character is likely to talk more than do or feel. This may be appropriate for some characters but certainly not all.

Train the chest with the breath to be able to reveal the rise and fall of victory or defeat, to fall in relief, grief or in love. Develop the supple expansion of joy, awe, hope, rage and courage. Craft the skill to contract in fear, consternation and contemplation or struggle for balance in excitement or anxiety. Cultivate the spine separately from the shoulders and clavicle.

Here is an exercise to help train an awareness and flexibility of the IAC:

Begin with a partner to help experience how much flexibility you have. Person 'A' places the fingertips of one hand on the front center of the chest of Person 'B,' and with the other hand on the spine in the back, between the shoulder blades. This helps 'B' become aware of the malleability of the area. "B" now wraps his/her arms across the chest, around to the back allowing the spine to curve forward. 'A' should be able to feel the curve increase.

Release and feel the curve adjust. Now have 'B' arch by bringing the elbows as far back as possible. Try to touch the elbows behind the back. The spine should arch forward. Repeat this several times in its most exaggerated form, until 'B' can sense the movement without the aid of 'A.' Swap tasks.

When this flexibility is achieved, begin to lessen the engagement of the arms, and separate the engagement of the shoulders, while seeking to retain the spinal movement.

Ultimately, the aim is for this central area to be able to push or pull, expand or contract, rise or fall, in subtle and bold ways, visible from all directions.

By training in this way, audience from any direction will sense the life of the character. Their own breathing will entrain with you and their emotional life will follow suit.

Additional points in the Chekhov Technique that are useful include special development of the legs as expressive means. Many actors are disconnected from their pelvis to their feet. That part of the body spends most of its time keeping the actor's "face off the floor" or on the chair. How can the pelvis, legs and feet reveal character and objective? The need for a good answer to this question is multiplied in its importance in alternative staging forms. When the audience is generally guaranteed to see more of an actor's profile and back than in a proscenium (or in film), we must insure the cast is able to radiate images in a constant stream of artistic impulses in any direction and from all body parts.

I mention film here because most of our audiences today are accustomed to watching and listening to things from the image of a screen (and actors are often trained to replicate that in performance). The proscenium stage most emulates that audience–artist relationship of a screen. To change that relationship while maintaining, and preferably, deepening the connection, requires heightened awareness of all body parts. Weaknesses in fully engaged physicality are often overlooked in a proscenium structure. Chekhov's exercises build performer adaptability by engaging stronger physicality, helpful to staging in all forms.

Motivating technically required blocking is the joint task of the actor and the director. Understanding the rhythm of the scene is the most important part of creating the illusion that a shift in position is needed by the players to express themselves to each other. Blocking one part of the audience too long in the juiciest moments may cause your audience to disconnect from the story, feeling sorry for the seat they got.

The more fully the actors are radiating through their entire being and the more powerful the atmosphere, the less this problem will exist. Too much movement will distract, not enough will frustrate.

Tips for Directors and Designers

In NTS, designers and directors will need to consider the line, flow and movement of a piece from the set design to the costume, props, lighting and sound to even the hair, makeup and microphone placement on the actors and props. Costuming can often become the singular most visually dynamic element as audiences frequently gaze into other audience members, separated only by the costumed characters and low lying set pieces.

Directors need to hold safe the image that unites every element of the story. It is their task to keep evaluating all points of view to create the sense of Beauty, Ease, Entirety and Form in alternative forms of staging.

Above all, directing the cast to actively create a continuous flow charging the playing space with energy is the central path to engaging the soul of the audience. The atmosphere is what first greets the spectator and can linger with them for a lifetime.

Notes

1 Michael Chekhov, *To the Actor: On the Technique of Acting*. London: Routledge, 2002, p. 35.
2 Chekhov, *To the Actor*, p. 41.
3 Chekhov, *To the Actor*, p. 41.
4 Chekhov, *To the Actor*, p. 19.
5 Chekhov, *To the Actor*, p. 10.
6 Chekhov, *To the Actor*, p. 70.

Arcadia by Tom Stoppard. In the round production directed by Anjalee Deshpande Hutchinson, lighting and set design by Karel Blakeley, costume design by Katrin Naumann. Le Moyne College, 2005.

Credit: Mark Hutchinson

Credit: drawing courtesy of Pablo Guerra-Monje

3

DISCOVERING THE DELIGHT

Sometimes as artists and academics we lift the idea of art onto a pedestal, valuing the content ingrained in its meaning over the way that content is delivered. A witty student of mine named Mukta calls this 'Urt.' Not quite art, but wanting so badly to call itself art that it takes itself a little too seriously. The work becomes hollow or self-important or worst of all, boring. Entertainment is not the enemy of art. When did the idea of craftsmanship become so misconstrued? The true artist is one that considers deeply both the meaning of what they are expressing and the way in which they convey it. As performing artists, one of our tools is that of delight. We can engage an audience in many ways, challenge them intellectually, enrapture their emotions, provoke their sense of self, etc.

One of the traditional ways of engaging is to delight the audience.

Through the sheer craft of your performance, you can capture the audience's imagination and easily suspend their disbelief. One way to do this is to deeply immerse yourself in the work of creating/discovering a character. Through your acute attention to detail and your ability to highlight the extraordinary out of the ordinary, a kind of poetry emerges about who the character is. Your embodiment of this living poem can resonate deeply with an audience, as they recognize either themselves or each other in your gorgeously immaculate renderings of the people you play. To delight means to captivate, to charm, to thrill or to enchant. Developing your skills in these areas are paramount to working in non-traditional performances because they give your audience the gift of something new from every vantage point. When you deeply invest in the character, it will be easy to give each audience its own special gift of insight into who you are.

The first step to fully manifesting this idea is to engage the physical imagination. Michael Chekhov exercises are designed to give performers a chance to solve the question of who a character is through the body and then to analyze their intentions only after some physical discoveries have been made. The traditional Western approach to character study is the other way around, finding the objective intellectually and then working to find ways to manifest the intellectual discoveries through the body. Have you ever heard an actor say, 'I know what my character's objective is, I just can't seem to figure out how to show that' or 'I know what I want to show but I'm just not sure how to do that' or maybe 'I can see what my body should do in my mind, I just can't get it to do that when I'm working.' These are all symptoms of the 'working from the intellect first' approach which doesn't always provide satisfying results in rehearsal, and in performance can lead to a predictable, calculated or less creative choices and interpretations. The key to character exercises through the Chekhov Technique is to embrace what shows up in the body, creating many different kinds of movements and then seeing which one really resonates with the actor for the character. It doesn't actually have to make intellectual sense. It just has to feel exciting and interesting in the body. This kind of approach can lead to some unique engaging kinds of discoveries that will manifest in detailed character renderings, as well as help actors break out of their own habitual acting and movement patterns which may not serve the character.

Exercises 3.1 and 3.2 Qualities of Movement and Elemental Physicality with Music

Based on MC's Tool Quality of Movement

Humans as a species love to categorize all things. From the moment we can speak and give names to the objects around us, we do so. One reason is to be able to communicate, another is to feel as though we know something more deeply once we decide we know what kind of thing it is that we are dealing with. Categorization is also one way we love to find out about ourselves, and others. Haven't you ever taken an internet quiz on what kind of Avenger you'd be? How about what house you'd belong to at Hogwarts? Or perhaps which district you'd be from in the Hunger Games, which faction you'd belong to in Divergent, what Pokemon you would be? We love categorization and somehow it gives us insight into who a person is, how a person behaves and what a person does. In the Chekhov Technique, there are many different exercises which help you choose and more deeply investigate your character through the use of categories. One such exercise explores physicality through a set of categories known as 'movement qualities,' which are the essential or defining characteristics of how a person moves in the world. Sculpting/molding, which we explored in Chapter 2, is one of the four movement qualities in Chekhov's work.

One way to use the Chekhov Quality of Movement exercises (QOM) is to employ the use of categorization. Taking Chekhov's four qualities of movement (Sculpting/Molding, Floating/Flowing, Flying and Radiating) and allowing one type of movement quality to be the main root of a character's physicality can be very useful in portraying a rich physical presence on the stage. Chekhov also allows for the physicality to enhance the inner life of the character as well: "When you are thoroughly familiar with these four kinds of movement (Molding, Floating, Flying and Radiating), and are able to fulfill them easily, try to reproduce them in your imagination only."[1] The usefulness of actors having 'flying thoughts' or a 'radiant desire' cannot be overestimated. Allowing the physical to lead the internal process of character building can be a glorious revelation. The following exercise introduces these qualities as the elements they relate to and allows the actor to play with the imagery of the element as an entry point.

The four movement exercises (Sculpting/Molding, Flying, Floating/Flowing and Radiating) that Chekhov uses to describe choices in physicality are known as the 'Qualities of Movement' exercises. Each specific kind of movement has the potential to fulfill a character's physical potential onstage, once you decide which one (or which combination) best suits your character.

If your actors are new to Chekhov, you can begin by letting actors explore each QOM movement before introducing music with this first exercise.

Coaching Qualities of Movement and Elemental Physicality

Based on Chekhov's Quality of Movement Exercises

Objective: To explore new ways to move and make discoveries about the character's physicality and self.

Coach:

- In this next section we will be moving through the space exploring different kinds of movements, in particular movements that play with degrees of resistance in the space and air around you.
- As we move, allow yourself to explore movement in every part of your body from your arms, legs, fingers and toes to your belly, back, butt, back of neck, ears, etc. Keep changing and exploring new ways to move through the space—don't get stuck in one kind of movement for too long.
- Feel free to also include your face, eyes and expression. In the end, even try to imagine the quality of movement affecting your very thought processes.
- Make sure to try different levels and when appropriate different tempos!

At this point have everyone move around the space just generally noting their energy and then maybe pulling up by placing their center in their IAC as discussed in 'Advice from the Pros' in Chapter 2. Then when ready, begin:

Coach:

- *Imagine you are moving through hard clay leaving 'carvings' in the space around and behind you. Using every part of your body, explore sculpting through the world, leaving trails everywhere you go.*

Note: Be sure to continue to push everyone to try different things if they get stuck, to use more of their body if they are really only

moving with hands and arms, to engage the face if they have for-
gotten it—and even the eyes: 'Can you carve with a look?'

Coach (giving them a little time with each Molding image):

- Now imagine that you are moving, molding through earth, a
  little easier to move through but still resistant. Now mud. Now
  honey. Now sand. Continue to leave honey trails that form and
  un-form. Now the space is changing but you are more in control
  of it.
- Imagine that your molding becomes more of a slicing through
  space. How can you slice with your back, your shoulders, your
  smile?
- Now allow that slicing to become more of a chopping. Chis-
  eling. Hacking. Whittling. Dicing. Shaping. Engraving. Light
  tracing.

Note: Going from images (move through honey) to verbs (whittle/
trace/chop) can help different kinds of actors who are working
together. There are so many different kinds of ways to approach the
work, and so many different kinds of learners/artists that encouraging diverse approaches seamlessly within the same exercise both
validates the neurodiversity of your ensemble as well as encouraging ways in which to grow their ability to work together.

*Coach (now moving on, giving them a little time with each Floating
image/idea/verb):*

- Now imagine that your molding slowly begins to transform.
  Imagine the space around you becoming less resistant and
  more fluid. Imagine a current moving all around you and let
  yourself be carried by the movement.
- Allow yourself to float. Just float. Float downstream. Float as if
  you were in outer space. Float like a soap bubble. Float like a
  blimp. Float like a dead body on the sea.
- Allow the floating to take different forms in your body. Allow your
  back, chest and neck to float like seaweed moving back and

(continued)

(continued)

forth, swayed by the current. Allow the sway to move into your legs, thighs, knees and calves. Now allow yourself to become unmoored from the ocean floor and allow the water to just carry you in swirls around the ocean. Let that transform into a dandelion seed floating through a summer day. What does that image do to your breath? Your gaze? Your thoughts?

Coach (now moving on, giving them a little time with each Flying idea/image/verb):

- Now allow that floating movement to begin to get more free. A rushing upward. The feeling of flying. How does your body fly through the space?
- Now let yourself fly like a bird. Fly like a bat. How is that different? Fly like a jet plane, a paper airplane. A butterfly.
- Let yourself flutter like a butterfly. Buzz like a bee. Flit like a fly, a moth, a wasp, a hummingbird.
- Exploring flying with different parts of your body. Can you fly with your ears? Flutter with your toes? Flit with your eyes? Buzz with your thoughts?
- Let yourself fly into a rage. Fly off the handle. Fly away from it all.
- Now soar. High above it, like an eagle. Soar.

Note: The chances are that exploring flying movements will make your actors want to move fast and only explore one kind of tempo. I like to end on something different to give the actors a sense of options. Just as there are different kinds of 'sub-objectives' available within a strong objective (or action verb if you prefer), these four qualities of movement are Archetypal Qualities and allowing actors to choose one kind of movement from which to explore character doesn't have to limit their movement choices. Structure can actually allow for more freedom by giving actors a place to start. If an actor decides their character's movement quality is flying, that is a starting point from which multiple different interpretations can arise, because the teenager with manic flying thoughts about relationships vs. the teenager whose heart soars when thinks about his crush can provide two very different meaningful interpretations of the same character, and these can both originate from and add to exciting revelations in physicality for the actor.

Coach (now moving on, giving them a little time with each Radiating idea/image/verb):

- Now imagine the feeling of soaring begins to transform into a feeling of warmth emanating from your chest. Deep radiating warmth that begins to emerge from your chest forward. Imagine a searchlight shining light from your chest, shining in everywhere you go. Now imagine that light emanates from every pore of your body filling the space around you with brightness. Where you go, the dark disappears. You are the light.
- Now allow that light is like the sun. Imagine shining sunlight wherever you go. Imagine sunlight in the palms of your hands, the small of your back, the arches of your feet. Explore moving with the quality of radiant sunlight.
- Now allow that sunlight to become moonlight. What has changed? What is different? Can you radiate moonlight from your legs, your lips, your breath?
- Now allow the moonlight to become a laser beam shooting out with your every turn. Now radiate a golden halo around your head. Now radiate stars through your smile.
- Now allow yourself to move like a crackling fire in a fireplace. Now a house fire—how is that different? Forest fire. Campfire. Candles in church. A birthday candle.

Note: With the movement quality of radiation, I find imagery to be sometimes more effective because radiation has the least resistance in all the movement qualities so it is hard to imagine how to literally affect the space around you without an image to begin. So this exercise begins to take on multiple imagistic levels. When people ask about radiation, I often speak about people who walk into a room and instantly make people want to come to them, or perhaps make the room feel warmer or brighter. Or the other extreme, people who make you uncomfortable just by entering the space. It is a quality

(continued)

(*continued*)

of movement, a way that they move and how the can change the energy in a room as they enter. If an actor is playing someone who has to be 'a creepy man on a subway,' the tool of Radiation can be extremely useful, providing the actor with such prompts to explore as 'radiate a burning hatred of women' or 'radiate sexual hunger and the desire to taste.' Clearly, safe space boundaries must be observed but the physical possibilities are undeniably exciting and the range of imagistic choices are endless.

Continue to coach (giving them a little time with each Radiating idea/image/verb):

- Now imagine the light you radiate begins to transform. It has ability to takes on many forms. Let the first one be sunshine, let yourself radiate sunshine as you walk into a room. Say hello to people as you walk by. Radiate sunshine as you greet people.
- Now let that transform into sweetness. How is that different? Radiate sweetness with every move of your body. Now radiate saccharine. It is like sweetness but not quite real. A fake sweetness. Now radiate poison. Can you radiate poison with your walk? Your breath? You eyes? Your smile? Your thoughts?
- Now radiate giddiness, you just can't keep the smile, giggle, bubbling laughter in.
- Radiate trust. Strength. Longing. Fierce desire.
- Radiate the feeling of being lost. Being better than. Being free. Being trapped.
- Radiate celebration. Radiate emptiness.
- Radiate hope.

Note: With the movement quality of radiation, I also like to end on hope. These exercises can become so visceral, so fully engaging that if we must end and the ending leaves the actors in a place of vulnerability, I believe it is best to end positive.

Coach:

- Once the exercise has ended, spend time discussing with the actors what they experienced. Ask what surprised them and what they found in terms of physicality. If used in a rehearsal process, be sure to ask if any character discoveries and/or connections could be made from the work.

- A shortened version of this same exercise could be used once a week with a direct prompt to 'explore how your character would move as in each quality.' This has the added bonus of forcing the actor to 'try on' all four qualities for their character before making a choice. Often the movement quality that is chosen was not the one the actor would have chosen intellectually and the freedom to let the character 'show up' through the movement can be really valuable.

One last note in this section: When referring back to the original books by Michael Chekhov, it is important to note that, due to the complicated business of translating Chekhov's works to English, certain words are repeated in different ways according to different exercises. In the QOM exercises, Floating or Flowing refers to being moved by the current around you and Radiating refers to emanating a kind of light from within. Sculpting and Molding are also used interchangeably.

In this next exercise, we approach the QOM through music. This wonderful way into the process allows for a more visceral response from the actors than traditional coaching, and can sometimes step the work up to the next level.

Actors engaged in 'Elemental Physicality with Music'.
Credit: Gordon Wenzel

Coaching Elemental Physicality with Music

Based on Chekhov's Quality of Movement Exercises

Objective: To explore new ways to move and make discoveries about the character's physicality and self through music.

This exercise requires a night of creativity on your part in order to make it successful. Before the exercise begins, prepare a playlist of different kinds of music. This playlist will be exploring Qualities of Movement, but from the standpoint of the elements to which the movements correspond. There should be at least three from each different category: Earth, Water, Air, Fire. Generally speaking:

- *Earth* is more staccato, more stylized, heavy or premeditated kind of music. Listen for deep percussive drums or a didgeridoo. Earth is connected to the QOM of Sculpting/Molding.
- *Water* is more legato, less structured and/or loose and flowing. Look for strings like harp or violin. Or flute. Water is connected to the QOM of Flowing.
- *Air* is heightened, either quick or slow but direct and open in its approach. It may be lyrical or even chaotic. Look for cellos or flute. Air is connected to the QOM of Flying.
- *Fire* is bright and in a way forceful or deeply soulful—sort of epic in its sound. Perhaps it is punctuated with silence. Look for xylophone, bells, timpani. Or trumpets. Fire is connected to the QOM of Radiating.

If we were looking just at soundtracks composed by Danny Elfman here are some examples:
Earth:

- *Beetle Juice*
- *Hulk*
- *Dark Man*
- *Nightmare before Christmas*
- *Planet of the Apes*

Water:

- *Edward Scissorhands*
- *Big Fish*
- *Dolores Clayborn*
- *Charlotte's Web*

Air:

- *Mission Impossible*
- *Spiderman*
- *A Civil Action*
- *Men in Black*
- *Corpse Bride*
- *The Simpsons' theme song*
- *Alice in Wonderland*

Fire:

- *Batman*
- *Dick Tracy*
- *Red Dragon*
- *Sleepy Hollow*
- *The Terminator: Salvation*

Granted the above selections are very subjective and cases can be made for moving some fire to the earth category, some water to the air category and vice versa. Yet the music will evoke a feeling from your actors and by playing many of these in a row and asking actors to call out the type of element or movement associated with these soundtracks is a fun way to begin this exercise (even before you ask them to get up on their feet!) Most of these are readily available on YouTube as compilations.

As you choose the music you will use for the movement component of the exercises, be sure to make selections that feel contradictory in each category. A quick classical piano and a heavy slow didgeridoo for earth. A sweet happy pop song and a maybe a sad

(continued)

(continued)

Actors engaged in 'Elemental Physicality with Music'
Credit: Gordon Wenzel

lilting flute for water. Etc. These categories should not feel completely positive or negative, or easily definable. Some birds soar and some flutter but they are all birds and move in a somewhat similar way. All the categories have subcategories—challenge yourself to find them! Other alternative ideas include:

- Looking for soundscapes instead of composed music.
- Incorporating vocals that don't have words or in other languages.
- Utilizing live musicians (as Michael Chekhov himself did!).
- Utilizing live vocalists.

Choose the clearly identifiable songs for the beginning, save some more ambiguous ones for the end. (Although this is primarily an exploration exercise for the classroom or rehearsal hall, if you have a sound designer who likes to experiment and/or if you have a clear idea of what you want a show to sound like in terms of design, you could also incorporate production sound design into this work.) How long each piece should be depends on how long a time you have in rehearsal for this exercise. Half an hour can produce some very powerful work. That means 1–2 minutes per song max. Create your playlist and make sure you have a way to play, pause and control volume in your rehearsal space. You want to have a way to lower the volume and coach when directions are needed. Now you are ready to begin.

Coach (before you start the music):

- I'm going to play you some music! And I want you to move to the music. Imagine that the music defines the world around you and that you are a native of that world. Born in it. Raised in it. Comfortable with it, the music is your home. Allow yourself to move in a way that is native to the world of this music.
- Your movement is not dance per se, although you can play with that if you like. Moreover, it is how people move through life who feel the rhythm of this music in their bones. Explore how a person who 'lives' their life in this song (consciously or unconsciously) moves.
- Play with large abstract movements and then when you are comfortable, condense the movement in a more natural way to move around the space. A way of moving that defines who you are. How you sit. How you stand. How you see people, greet people.
- This music is neither negative nor positive. It just is. You decide how your body interprets it, how it feels to live there.
- As each piece of music begins, I'm going to give you an element. There will be four elements: Fire, Water, Air, Earth. Let the image connect to the music through your body.
- After we go through all four images, I will continue to give you different pieces of music. You decide which one of the four elements connects to the music that is played. Find the connections between the element you choose for the music through your body.
- Don't think! Your first impulse is right! Don't worry about what you look like or if you are doing this right. If you are doing it, then you are doing it right!
- When you are searching for the right element for a piece of music, stand still for a moment if you need to. Then when you find the element—move. Don't premeditate your movement, let your body tell you how to move. The music could be very different from the first music you connected to the element! That's okay. Trust your instincts!

(continued)

(*continued*)

- Each of the following pieces of music may relate to one of these four elements deeply. You decide which element belongs to which piece of music and then explore the physicality of both the music and the image of the element in concert with one another.
- Work in your own space and with your own body. Try to stay in your own experience right now.

Once the exercise begins, the actors will take it from there. At first you may need to coach them to make their choices bigger or more expansive in order to find new patterns of movement. Alternatively, you may need to ask them to condense it or to make it more natural should you find something you like that you would like to use in production. However, for the exercise, make sure they move through a range of levels and ranges of motion in order to give the actors the most in terms of opportunity for discovery.

Actors engaged in 'Elemental Physicality with Music'.
Credit: Gordon Wenzel

Coach:

- Don't get stuck! Try new things! When you find something you like you can play with it for a while but keep exploring.
- Make it bigger! More abstract!
- Condense it. Put it in your bones or behind your eyes—in your smile. Just as much energy but contained up and underneath.

Once the exercise is complete, ask the actors what songs, movements and images (flowing, flying, molding and radiating or water, air, earth, fire) felt most resonant for them. Ask them what movements felt natural and which did not. Ask them which movements/images might connect to their character and if they can think of other songs that might inspire physicality appropriate to their characters. Give them homework to find these songs, make them readily available to listen to at any time and play with movement in their bedrooms, as they walk across town or campus and in their daily lives. Ask them to listen to the music right before rehearsal so that they can hear it inside their heads when they begin the scene work. Ask them to explore how the music, image and movement change their physicality in the scene.

Exercise 3.3 The Rapture

Based on MC/NMCA's Tools Sister Sensations and Veiling

In Joseph Campbell's *The Power of Myth*, he states:

> People say that what we're all seeking is a meaning for life. I don't think that's what we're really seeking. I think what we're seeking is an experience of being alive, so that our life experiences on the purely physical plane will have resonance within our own innermost being and reality, so that we actually feel the rapture of being alive.[2]

Traditional American actor training has traditionally been about 'feeling' an emotion on the inside first and then showing it on the outside. The problems with finding and/or creating this kind of authentic deep emotion and then performing it (let alone replicating it over and over) has been documented time and again, one of the most notable renditions from the musical *A Chorus Line* with the song 'Nothing.'

But what if we started from the other way around. Let the body experience a physical sensation and then begin to create a detailed rendering of the kind of person who lives in that sensation much of the time—the sensation that resonates with the character's own innermost being and reality.

Michael Chekhov/NMCA Sister Sensations tools (the term 'sister' being a helpful NMCA mnemonic) do just that. They take the actor through a series of physical sensations and then ask the actor to find the one that resonates most deeply with their character.

Chekhov connects sensations to qualities as a means of accessing emotional states onstage. Mala Powers, a long-time student of Chekhov's, described how he clarified that connection through the idea of accessibility:

> Feelings cannot be commanded, they can only be coaxed. The means for coaxing up feelings are qualities and sensations. Qualities are immediately accessible to you—especially to your movements. You can immediately move your arms and hands with the quality of tenderness, joy, anger, suspicion, sadness, impatience, etc. even though you do not experience the feeling of tenderness, joy or anger. After moving with one of these qualities, sooner or later you will observe that you are experiencing the sensation of tenderness, and very soon the sensation will call up a very true emotion or feeling of tenderness within you.[3]

Even if true emotion or feeling were not to arise within the actor, the quality of the movement would be enough to create the sensation within the audience. When working with creating movements through qualities or imagined sensations, the resulting physicality can produce an easily perceivable bridge to the emotional life of a character which is then accessible to the spectator. What a huge gift—especially for the audience of a NTS production, where physicality is sometimes the most visible bridge.

Another excellent connected tool Chekhov employed was called 'Veiling.' Veiling encouraged actors not to 'dial down' energy to match the style of a play, film or TV project. Rather, he asked them to concentrate and contain the energy, which in turn would resonate palpably with an audience. Mala Powers described Chekhov as a man who was interested in exploring the full 'scope, depth and power' of emotional range and how turning energy down was never an option:

> Actors often hear the admonition "Do Less." Chekhov would have said "Do more but veil it." In other words, increase the strength

of your radiation, call up the emotions that you are filled to the brim with, and then imagine a soft gossamer "veil" descend upon you, veiling your expression. If you try to "do less" you may kill the emotion. The image of the veil however, when evoked many times, in many different highly emotional moments, leads to great power. It results in an economy of expression and real "presence", which the audience experiences.[4]

In this set of exercises, we find physicality through the active pursuit/ evocation of sensations, allowing them to energetically communicate what the character is feeling through movement.

Coaching The Rapture

Based on Michael Chekhov/National Michael Chekhov Association's 'Sister Sensations' Work and Veiling Exercises

Objective: To explore physical sensations to connect to and present physicalized emotional states onstage.

Coach Balancing:

- Ask your actors to begin to imagine they are walking on a tightrope. If you have a low wall or something else that the actors can actually balance on (safely), that is an even better way to play with this idea.
- Have them walk on this wall (or imaginary tightrope) and work hard at balancing. Talk to the ensemble while they are working to get them thinking about what balancing feels like.
- Modern society makes 'balance' seem like a positive well-being, but actual balancing requires work. You have to fight to keep balancing.

  - There is a tension in the body.
  - Begin to fall over to one side—then recover!
  - What is the sensation of getting back to the feeling of balancing when you've temporarily lost it?
  - What is the sensation of almost losing it?

(continued)

(*continued*)

- What does it feel like to live a balancing lifestyle? Balancing your inner and outer worlds?
- What is the difference between an active state of balancing and the passive state of 'balanced.'
- Imagine that there is never a passive state for the balancer. 'Balanced' is the goal you strive for but is always just out of reach.

Coach Falling:

- Next have your actors fall. Only so far as they can land or catch themselves safely. Perhaps have them fall forward as far as they can safely do and still be able to catch themselves. Talk to the ensemble, while they are working to get them thinking about what falling feels like:

  - How far can you go?
  - What does it feel like to fall forward with each step?
  - What kind of person feels this sensation all the time?
  - Is there anything fun or exciting about it?
  - Is there anything scary or uncomfortable about it?
  - Try falling to the side. Try falling backwards. Try falling with your eyes closed. Exciting and fun or terrifying and awful?

- If you would like to add partnered trust falls here, or even a fall off a table backwards with ensemble catching the participant (be sure you know how to do this correctly to avoid injury)—it can help the process.

Coach Floating:

- Now have your actors begin to imagine the feeling of floating, or floating away. Have them move about the room floating. Talk to the ensemble, while they are working to get them thinking about what floating feels like:

  - Think about an upward motion lifting you from the inside at all times
  - What does floating around the room feel like?

- Is it fun and relaxing?
- Is it kind of disconcerting and uncomfortable?
- Allow yourself to feel the feeling of not being in control, letting any little stimulus move you.
- Bumping into someone changes your direction, feeling of wind on your face changes your direction, a breeze, a bright light, a sharp piece of architecture.
- Try not to predict when something will change your movement—just let the outside influence where you go.

Continue coaching:

- Once they have completed all three sensations, have the ensemble come together and speak about their discoveries. What does it feel like to Float, Fall or Balance? Where are people most comfortable?
- Then move to character work, asking them—what kind of a person is always fighting for balance? Anyone you know? How about falling—what kind of person is constantly falling through their life? Falling into trouble? In love? What about floating— know anyone who just goes with the flow and floats from one moment to the next?

A Note on Floating

Sometimes one component of the Sister Sensations tool gets confused with the Qualities of Movement tool because 'flowing' from QOM is sometimes translated as 'Floating'—so the same words are used for both exercises. To distinguish the two, consider that QOM exercises deal with the idea of resistance to movement while sensations exercises deal more with the idea of gravity, which is the heart of this tool. Falling is yielding to gravity. Balancing is teetering. Floating is freedom from gravity. Flowing with the current (QOM) is different than floating weightlessly (SS).

(continued)

(continued)

Archetypal examples from TV shows or popular films are helpful with sensations. You can use the example below (which I researched with my knowledgeable 15-year-old daughter Kate) or use your own:

Harry Potter
Balancing—Hermione
Floating—Ron
Falling—Harry

Star Wars
Balancing—Darth Vader, Leia, C3P0
Floating—Luke, Yoda
Falling—Anakin, R2D2, Han Solo

How I Met Your Mother
Balancing—Robin
Floating—Lily and Marshal
Falling—Ted and Barney

Grey's Anatomy
Balancing—Miranda, Callie, Christina
Floating—George, McDreamy, McSteamy, Arizona
Falling—Meredith, Alex

Weeds
Balancing—Celia, Dean
Floating—Andy, Shane
Falling—Nancy, Silas, Doug

Big Love
Balancing—Nicolette, Bill
Floating—Margene, Ben
Falling—Barbara, Sara

It is also helpful to ask if anyone has an example from their friends, family, professors—and to share.

Ideally, present this exercise with full explanation once, then immediately have them get on their feet to try it again. Have them carry the question of their character just barely into the exercise to see what arises. Ask them to ask themselves, what if my character was a balancing person—what would that feel like? Falling? Floating? Connect the sensation to their journey throughout the play.

Like the 'Qualities of Movement', Michael Chekhov's 'Sensations' ask actors to categorize their characters. They do this by 'trying on' or feeling the essential sensations of these three archetypal ways of being and then playing with the potential inner experience of the character to influence an external physicalization of the character. Be sure to encourage the actors to play with the sensations and the resulting physicality as large and abstractly as possible to begin so they can find the greater arc of movement before they begin to distill down to their more realistic versions, depending on the style of the production. At this point we bring in the tool of Veiling.

Always find the largest and most expansive version of the physicality before revealing less and less through levels of veiling depending on the style (commedia or farce vs. melodrama or realism). When an actor does eventually reveal less of the larger movement, the energy of the movement is just as powerful up and underneath and only the shape of the revelation is changed. A valiant chaotic struggle in the body may then only be revealed through the eyes (for film) but the struggle is no less powerful, it is just contained. Encourage your actors to experiment as physically broadly and expansively as they can so that they can find the deepest sensations of their characters' innermost being. This being can be directly influenced by their deepest desires, fears, hopes and dreams. Let the physicality reveal the character's psychology and their experience of being alive. Then try again using this veiling exercise:

Coach:

- On your own move around the space trying out each of the three sensations independent of the character.

(continued)

(continued)

- When you feel you have unpacked a bit about what the feeling of the sensation is in your body, try on each sensation with your character in mind. Imagine that character as a balancing, floating or falling kind of person.
- Be careful that you do not attach a positive or negative association to these sensations or any particular judgment on the character through these sensations. Just let yourself imagine your character feeling the sensations and ask yourself which sensations are the most familiar to your character. What sensation are they most comfortable in—where do they 'live'?

After a few moments of letting them play, coach:

- Pick one of the three sensations to play with for your character. Imagine that there is a scale of one to seven on how much your character reveals (consciously or unconsciously) about the inner sensation she/he feels underneath everything that is going on in her/his day: seven is large and abstract, the biggest possible physicality of what is going on in regards to the sensations your character feels everyday; one is the same energy as seven, just contained, beneath the surface—but radiating out energetically all around.
- Do not ignore your legs and the bottom half of your body! The energy should be up and underneath but low and underneath as well: full body movement even when it is completely veiled.
- When you are completely veiled: this should feel like a person you can see in everyday life and unless you took a second look you would not necessarily see the sensations they are feeling. But they are still feeling those big feelings underneath. Now move around the room as your character exploring the sensation you chose to play with today.

Coach as they move, selecting numbers:

- Reveal what's beneath the surface at a two
- at a six

- at a three
- at a one
- at a seven, etc.

If there is time, it is nice to allow half the ensemble to watch the other half during this exercise and then switch. This will allow your actors to see how the large abstract movements still emerge in the veiled expression of them. If you do this, end with one and then ask them to come to a point of stillness or a pause and send what they are feeling out into the audience. Hold them there for at least three seconds and then release. Especially useful in NTS productions, ask them to stand with their back or side to the audience and repeat the exercise. When both halves have gone, circle your ensemble together and ask what they either felt or saw. Ask them specifically what they noticed about each other when they were in the audience and actors were radiating out into the audience. Most likely your audience members will affirm that the radiation of what is beneath the surface is a very powerful tool in communicating to spectators what the character is feeling and/or going through without the actor having to physically 'show' a thing. This vibrant energetic performance quality is exactly the inner muscles your actors will need to build as they get more and more proficient at performing vibrantly in non-traditionally staged and performed productions.

Exercise 3.4 The Trinity of Psychology:
Thinking, Feeling, Willing

Based on MC's Tool Character Spheres

Chekhov's work on what he calls "The threefold form of the human body"[5] refers to his interpretation of Rudolph Steiner's art of 'Eurythmy' (a kind of movement exploration and art form) for the actor. A part of this work divides the sections of the human body into three regions which house three different kinds of energy: a thinking force, a feeling force and a will force. Focus on anyone of these areas communicates a kind of unconscious preference in the character, communicated through the body. Each area of the body also comes with a particular kind of movement which 'reads' to the audience what the character values as well as how they live their life.

Mala Powers described working with Chekhov using the energies attached to these areas of the body as a starting point in all character work:

> Chekhov would begin to ask questions. The first was always "Is this a predominantly Thinking Character, a Feeling Character or a Will Character?" . . . When acting, it is quite valuable to know whether you are working with a character who has strong Will forces and relatively little intellectual power or one who has a strong Feeling life but little ability to take hold of his Will forces.[6]

The tool of isolating and exploring the region or sphere of the body that a character naturally moves from can reflect who that character is, particularly if actors explore the sphere through the kinds of movements associated with that area. In this exercise, Wil Kilroy offers specific movement patterns associated with each sphere, giving actors a way to explore full body movement that expresses innermost nature.

Coaching The Trinity of Psychology

Based on Chekhov's Ideas of Character Spheres

By Wil Kilroy

Objective: Actors explore characterization via thought, feelings and desire as they continue expanding their comfort zone, expressing in all directions of the space.

Coach the Thinking exercise:

- Initially actors are asked to compute a mathematical challenge—multiply 468 by 116 or divide 4,588 by 3. Immediately the thinking process will be engaged and you might even notice fingertips tapping on the head and strongly focused eyes.

Now the actors will have an idea of what it feels to be a character that is cerebral—constantly viewing the world via their thinking forces.

- Actors are now asked to walk around the space walking in very straight lines and when turning to make precise right angles. At the same time ask them to tap their index fingers to their foreheads, and imagine that all of their action originates from the brain. Actors can then begin to improvise with one another, keeping this specific and clearly exaggerated focus—but purposeful to be in touch with the thinking force. When speaking actors are coached to 'think' about each word and each sound, and to speak with clear precision. Actors could think about a future plan together, or solve a challenge, being sure to keep the linear actions with the pointing fingers and the rest of the body.

Actors engaged in a 'Thinking Movements' exercise.
Credit: Gordon Wenzel

Coach the Feeling exercise:

- Actors are instructed to bring to mind something they love—someone or something very near and dear to them. Quickly the body will soften and hands may even go to the heart in a curved gesture. Now the actors are experiencing a focus on the feeling forces, centered in the heart area.
- Actors are now instructed to move through the space, but rather than the linear movement they created while thinking, now their movement should be soft and curving, with open palms and

(continued)

(continued)

gestures staying in the 'heart zone'—the mid-section of the body. Actors now improvise with each other by sharing some-thing sweet and special from their life—real or imagined—while maintaining open palms and curving gestures centered in the heart area. While speaking, the focus is now on having very open and slightly elongated vowel sounds to encourage feel-ings to be expressed.

Coach the Will Force exercise:

- Actors are now asked to remember when they were five years old and wanted to get their way. Encourage the stomping of feet, and the flailing of limbs in all directions with guttural sounds, perhaps chanting "I want it!" From a juvenile outlook as a start, the actors will now be experiencing the will force.
- Actors are now asked to walk in the space, without any specific pattern but in a more erratic fashion—in a line, then a circle, then a reverse, while feeling power in the hip and groin area—known as the seat of the will force. Hands should remain closed with just the thumbs protruding, and gestures staying low—parallel to the hip area. Actors now improvise with each other by talking about something they are going to *do*, and allowing their speech to be more guttural, with perhaps the stereotype of a tough New Yorker. Therefore actors can be sharing what they are 'gonna' do with 'dese' and 'dose' guys.

Actors engaged in a 'Thinking vs. Feeling' exercise.
Credit: Gordon Wenzel

Note from Wil: One aspect of Michael Chekhov's technique is what he noted as 'jewelry.' During all exercises and improvisations, be aware of a surprising, sparkling moment—a jewel—that might stand out. Remember that 'jewel' and put it away in your box of precious items to be pulled out when it corresponds with a current or future character.

Exercise 3.5 Stupid, Fat and Smelly: Imaginary Body Breath Work

Based on MC's Tool Character Spheres

In this next set of exercises, Samantha Norton builds on the tools explored in the previous thinking/feeling/willing exercises by Wil Kilroy. In Sam's exercise, we explore these same ideas through the voice. She uses the MC tool of Character Spheres to explore breath and sound as well as the ability to express character through connected vocal work. Indeed, she examines voice and breath as an extension of the physical 'Three-Fold Form' of the body.

Coaching Stupid, Fat and Smelly

Inspired by Chekhov's Ideas of Character Spheres

By Samantha Norton

The real beauty of our art, if based on the activity of the creative individuality, is constant improvisation.[7]

Before we utter a word, our brain sends a signal to our vocal folds (chords) to begin speaking. Along with that signal, our brain and body are preparing for that utterance. So how we breathe is very important. For everyday use, our spontaneous breathing and speaking goes unnoticed, unless we are in distress. With actors and singers, however, we must be conscious of our breathing and the 70 muscles used to engage in speaking. Many vocal practitioners follow a

(continued)

(*continued*)

series of breathing exercises and vocalizations in a repetitive drill format. I argue that this method, even when done accurately, is missing key element—*images*. This is where Michael Chekhov steps in. In the spirit of the Michael Chekhov tool Character Spheres of Thinking, Feeling and Willing, we explore images and breath/voice exercises that focus on releasing areas of the Head, Torso and Groin. Anjalee and I came upon three exercises demonstrating breath and voice release in the Head, Torso and Groin regions. We call these exercises: STUPID, FAT and SMELLY. Anjalee suggests that these words are also what actors (and many non-actors) fear. Nobody wants to be perceived as stupid, fat or smelly. The fear of these kinds of physical 'expressions' limits our ability to release tension. These exercises help 'let go' of those specific kinds of tension in order to fully access breath and voice capacity.

Coaching Stupid

Objective: This series of stretches and movements motivated by our imagination invites your students to experience what tension they may be carrying in their jaws. Our focus is to allow our imagination to release tension not a series of technical drills.

Coach:

- Ask your students to say 'duh' a few times. Ask them to show you the kind of 'duh' that is perceived as ignorant or stupid. Demonstrate for them as well. Ask them to observe their jaw by opening and closing it a few times. Is it tight? Loose? Can't tell? Let it be loose. Now, ask them to soften their eyebrows and say 'duh' a few times. Anything different? Next, ask them to say 'duh' with relaxed eyebrows, then with soft eyes.
- Now ask students to add awareness of the tongue by letting it be as lazy as possible. Hopefully, they are getting images in their mind of what it feels like and what they may look like in doing the exercise. If you have students who say they don't like to look stupid or lazy, reassure them that this is an exercise of awareness. If the class as a whole is feeling insecure, have them try the 'duh' exercise with their eyes closed.

- Soon they will start to feel a release at the hinges of the jaw, which is a relaxing down and back a bit. Many of us hold quite a bit of tension in our jaws so finding a release even for a moment can be heavenly. As for the tongue, the hardest working muscle in speaking and singing, it's just happy to flop along.

Note from Anjalee: As a person who suffers with Temporomandibular Joint Disorder or TMJ (deep tension within the muscles of the jaw), the 'Duh' exercise can be a less strenuous way to warm up and release tension than the familiar 'chew a big wad of gum' exercises that are common in academic theatre settings. Softening, rather than stretching the jaw hinges, especially when your physical therapist has told you to avoid gum, taffy, etc. can be a welcome way to warm up effectively without pain.

Coaching Fat

Objective: These next exercises encourage students to engage the breath more deeply and fully by relaxing the chest and belly with the aid of a rubber band.

Coach:

- Next, give your students each a sturdy (to avoid snapping injury) rubber band. Ask them to begin breathing as they expand and contract their rubber band with their hands. Have extras on hand for when some snap to keep the exercise going.
- Tell them to walk around and continue to expand and contract the rubber band with their hands in a variety of ways, imagining that their breath capacity is connected to this expansion and contraction. The breath is connected to the stretch and release of the band.
- While the actors continue to explore the stretching and contracting of the bands in a variety of shapes as well as tempos (defined as speed in this exercise) and rhythms (patterns), see if you (the facilitator) can observe where each breath is being initiated in the body. Ideally, the inhale begins below the

(continued)

(continued)

belly button. Often students hold tension by holding the breath mainly in the chest or shoulders. Point this out to students and ask them to expand the band slowly and 'down.'

- Tell them to relax the belly while they send their breath 'slow and down.' Tell them to imagine having a very big paunchy belly and ask them to breath into that jiggly place. Tell them to use the band to expand both vertically and horizontally across the chest and belly. If actors are hesitant to engage the belly (many actors just don't want to appear 'fat,' another good way to encourage lower breath is for them to lie on their back while they manipulate the rubber band.

- When they have explored for a while, ask the actors to come to a circle and have each actor demonstrate a breath/band movement that they found very satisfying. Everyone should copy the movement with their own band after the first person demonstrates 'trying it on' their own body. When everyone has demonstrated and been copied by the whole ensemble, ask actors to let go of the bands but try to keep the fuller breath and awareness.

Note from Anjalee: The fat exercise is also a great way to warm up privately before an audition. Having a tool such as a rubber band encourages deep breathing, expands and relaxes the belly and chest for more breath capacity and also allows the intellect a way to engage the physicality in a discreet way that can be used anywhere. Just bring a rubber band and wrap it around your wrist, use it and then put it back on your wrist when your name is called.

Coaching Smelly

Objective: Although it often brings up a wonderful ripple of giggles, learning to release our sphincter (imagined, real or both) is the focus of this exercise mined from my opera days. Letting the muscles 'down there' go gives your students a power source for the voice.

Coach:

- To begin, ask your students to take in a few easy breaths and then vocalize on 'aah,' 'ee,' 'oh' (your choice) while ascending a scale. Now, ask your students to tighten their sphincters singing the same scale. Next, ask them to release the tension for the vocalization. Finally, ask for the same breath and vocalization but encourage them to simulate the sensation of pushing their sphincter toward the floor (aka) 'going #2.'
- This is where giggles and sometimes fear come into play. If the latter happens, encourage the student to just work on the second part (the release of tension). The result of this experiment usually falls into this progression: tightening the 'bum' renders a thin or constricted sound, releasing the tension adds a warmer and sustained sound.
- The final pressing of the sphincter toward the floor exercise offers a powerhouse of sound especially for higher notes. The trick is to keep the power low and full of air so it doesn't stress the vocal folds. The sphincter exercise is great for the actor too, particularly when their character needs to yell.

Overall, all of these warm-ups give opportunities to use or release tension. I purposely avoid judging all tension as bad tension. We need some tension to stand, move, speak and create imaginary characters. I entertain the idea that the more we know about where the tension lies in our 'civilian' selves, the better chance we have to release unnecessary actor tension while 'reassigning' necessary tension to the areas that help tell our character stories most clearly.

The actor's conscious use of the character's breathing is especially helpful when performing in non-traditional performance spaces. To demonstrate this, have your actors act out the following two scenarios:

Scenario 1
You have arranged a surprise party for your best friend. You've been planning this event for several weeks and

(continued)

(continued)

everyone is here to celebrate. Suddenly, you hear the car
drive up, the door shuts, everyone hears the sound of the key
in the lock then, as the door opens, you . . .

Tell me, was there any point where the actors held their breath?
If yes, the audience is probably holding their breath too! How
did you use your breath when you said 'surprise!'? I would guess
that it was a free and full exhale of sound, yes? If we, as actors are
aware of the power breath, our audiences will physically experience the moment with us.

To add a bit of humor, do the exercise where the wrong person
enters. How did your students exhale then?

Inevitably a play will have two or more characters overlap-
ping or cutting off the other. The problem for many actors is
that once they have memorized the scene, they lose the natural breath pattern that can enhance the action. Have your
actors try this scenario with you or another actor acting as the
teacher:

Scenario 2
Your teacher has been looking for you, they're furious!
They have reason to believe you cheated on your exam.
When they see you, they are rapidly listing several examples of your cheating. Meanwhile, you're trying to get a
word in to tell your teacher that their son is in a terrible
fist-fight with another student outside.

Each time your actors tried to speak what happened to their
breath? Was it cut-off, were the breaths short or sharp? What did
their shoulders do? Did they move up or down? What would
that movement mean to the audience? Were the inhales/exhales
audible? If the actor was successful in getting a word in, how
did it sound; loud, sharp, a whisper? Every choice we make with
our breath and sound can be a clear physical connection for the
audience particularly if the only thing some of the audience is
seeing is the rise and fall of an actor's back.

Advice from the Pros: Directing on the Thrust Stage—The Two-Room vs. One-Room Concept

By Ed Menta

If the thrust or three-quarter stage has such a long history (ancient Greece, Elizabethan stages, even the classical Japanese Noh stage could be considered a sort of thrust), how can it be considered 'non-traditional staging'? In Chapter 1 of this volume, Professor Hutchinson argues—correctly, I believe—that the proscenium theatre has long been considered the de facto 'normal staging' of American theatre, due in great part to the proliferation of proscenium-style high school auditoriums. I would also argue that the cinema has helped to entrench many of the aesthetic concepts of proscenium theatre. The performers are on one side of the room and the audience is on the other.

The performance actions take place on a fairly 'flat' level—either behind the arch (or on the screen). The audience sits in neatly ordered horizontal rows and the 'good seats' are at the center and not the sides (a component, to be sure, from the legacy of the Italian Renaissance). The performers are lighted and the audience sits in the dark. And so on. As an MFA Directing student at the University of Connecticut in the late 1970s, my graduate adviser, Dr. John Herr, referred to such aspects of proscenium staging as 'the two room' concept, that is, the actors stay in their room, the audience stays in their room, and never the twain shall meet. The two-room concept has stayed with me all these years, in my own directing and teaching.

Ed Menta, Professor of Theatre Kalamazoo College.
Credit: Ed Menta

In fact, I would argue that much of the 'avant-garde' theatre of the last 75 years has been an effort to break the two rooms (or maybe unite them?): Jerzy Grotowski's and Richard Schechner's environmental theatre, Peter Brook and Andrei Serban's ritual stagings of *Orghast* and *Fragments of a Greek Trilogy*, even today's 'site-specific' theatre.

But of course there have been 'more traditional' ways to break the two rooms. After all, before the experimental theatre of the 1960s and 1970s, Margo Jones at Theatre 47 in Dallas and Zelda Fichandler at the Arena Stage in Washington DC popularized theatre in the round in the first wave of America's regional theatres. And Harold Prince's 'environmental staging' of the musical *Candide* was a landmark of the Broadway theatre.

I have taught at Kalamazoo College in Michigan since 1986, where I've had the pleasure of directing more than 30 plays on the thrust stage of the 300-seat Nelda K. Balch Playhouse.

Opened in 1977 and modeled after the main stage of the Stratford Festival in Ontario, The Playhouse—as we call it—was the first thrust theatre in the state of Michigan (or so we've always told everyone!). Staging so many productions there had led me to realize that I've finally proved John Herr's thesis: the best theatre takes place in one room—not two. Ideally, the performers and audience are *always* in the same room. When there is a full house in The Playhouse (which has not always been the case on our strong diet of Brecht, Strindberg, and Churchill—among others—over the years!), the audience sees themselves watching the actors in a three-dimensional view, as opposed to the flat

Building the Nelda K. Balch Playhouse, 1977.
Credit: Ed Menta, Kalamazoo College Archives

perspective of the proscenium. We are all in the same room—living and breathing with the performers.

Ironically, some of the 'rules' I've learned in staging plays in this theatre are just as particular and even stringent as those often associated with the proscenium stage: staging with diagonal angles (as opposed to having the stage picture parallel to the seat line), having the actors 'get their backs into the voms'—the house left and house right vomitoria, vaulted exits and entrances from within the audience seating—and a carefully planned groundplan in order to bring credibly the action downstage. Over the years, in the many guest directors we've invited to work in The Playhouse, I can always ascertain if they haven't worked much on a thrust, as the tendency is always to "push" the action upstage toward our proscenium arch—24 feet from the furthest downstage point of the tip of the stage.

Directors new to the three-quarter round are so concerned about sightlines of the left and right sections of the house that they unnecessarily place major scenes upstage, in effect creating a horizontal and 'flat' staging for the proscenium on a thrust stage. In fact, I can still remember the ripple of surprise and even admiration I elicited from my departmental colleagues when, for my first play at 'K,' a production of Eugene O'Neill's *Ah, Wilderness!*, I placed an armchair of the main living room set with its back to the center section of the audience, at the extreme down right vom corner of the stage! It wasn't brilliant of course, but I was trying to provide 'realistic' reasons for the characters to come downstage. Yet another irony in such carefully planned staging is that it all goes to waste if only the center section of the house fills! For 30 years, I've failed to convince audience members that sitting in the

Kalamazoo College Actors rehearsing on the Nelda K. Balch Stage.
Credit: Ed Menta

house left and house right sections—that is, 'the sides'—are actually the some of the best seats in the house.

But the logistical 'tricks of the trade' in directing on a thrust stage pale in comparison for the more organic reasons for doing so. As John Herr taught me so long ago, we're trying to make theatre where both performers and audience are in the same room, not two rooms, a key concept when actors deliver dialogue while facing upstage from any portion of the audience (I admit that several years ago, we made the decision to mic the major singers when we do musicals. But even with such technical amplification, the care of a detailed, precise staging becomes even *more* crucial as audiences need to be able to identify immediately who is singing or speaking, since the sound is now emanating from speakers in front of the stage and at the back of the house.). It's not enough to ask student actors 'to project' or speak louder; instead, we must remind them to share their scene with 'everyone in the room.' We can't complete the theatrical work of art until the audience is in the same room as the performers.

Notes

1 Michael Chekhov, *To the Actor: On the Technique of Acting*. London: Routledge, 2002, p. 13.
2 Joseph Campbell, *The Power of Myth*. New York: Anchor, 1991, p. 3.
3 Chekhov, *To the Actor*, p. xli.
4 Chekhov, *To the Actor*, p. 165.
5 Michael Chekhov, *On the Technique of Acting*. New York: Harper, 1993, p. 52.
6 Chekhov, *On the Technique of Acting*, p. 160.
7 Chekhov, *On the Technique of Acting*, p. 19.

Arcadia by Tom Stoppard. In the round production directed by Anjalee Deshpande Hutchinson, lighting and set design by Karel Blakeley, costume design by Katrin Naumann. Le Moyne College 2005.

Credit: Mark Hutchinson

Credit: drawing courtesy of Pablo Guerra-Monje

4

EMBODYING THREE-DIMENSIONAL RESONANCE

Avatar is a Hindu word that means 'the manifestation of the divine in physical form.' Currently in most Western countries it has many meanings, including the name of a popular James Cameron movie that my kids love (about humans living in alien bodies) and an excellent Nickelodeon series that our whole family loves (about a young boy reincarnated with the power of the divine within). To gamers, the word 'avatar' also means 'an icon or figure representing a real person in computer games, Internet forums, etc.' All these ideas work together when considering our work in expressing our internal innermost thoughts/desires/feelings through the physical body. We must always be working with the internal finding expression through the external and even more so in non-traditional staging.

Like most contemporary video games, NTS theatre requires a character that is defined three-dimensionally and from every angle. There is no hiding on the arena stage. You cannot wipe your nose upstage or 'play a secret game of tag' with your colleagues while phoning in the performance (Have you heard about this awful practice? Don't be one of those actors!). Arena staging means you are all in—100 percent. If you are creating a 'video-game' demon, the shape/texture/color of the muscles in the back are just as important as the face. So too must we seek to define our characters with a skillful hand from every vantage point. Yet not just that, we must also seek to manifest the most authentic, deeply meaningful and multilayered interpretation possible. We must manifest this artistic facet of the divine in all of its glory.

A Note on Divinity, Sin and Chekhov Technique

Chekhov (as well as his mentor Konstantin Stanislavski) studied Hinduism, along with Buddhism, during his time at the Moscow Art Theatre. Through his work with Leopold Sulerzhitsky, he studied yoga, prana and other spiritual practices common to Eastern religions. These influences impacted his work as well as his methodology and approach to character. In the Hindu religion, divinity is not always perceived as good and/or perfect. Hinduism argues that a tiger is not evil when it eats the deer. It is an animal, just as it is. It resides outside of judgment. Similarly, Chekhov promoted the ability to embrace our characters fully, even those that are reprehensible, terrifying, weak or cruel. He believed that our job as performers is not to judge those we play and that judgment was an inherently political rather than artistic act: "The Aim of our Creative Individuality is not to be confused with propaganda, which is preconceived and schematically devised and fixed expression."[1] He believed imposing a judgment on characters was not a true expression of the 'Higher Ego,' which is what Chekhov called the part of the artist that was most altruistically connected to the world and most able to fully embody characters onstage.

Chekhov believed that the strongest inspiration comes from a place of non-judgment:

The other attribute of creative feelings is that they are compassionate . . . Compassion may be called the fundamental of all good art because it alone can tell you what other beings feel and experience. Only compassion severs the bonds of your personal limitations and gives you deep access into the inner life of the characters you study, without which you cannot properly prepare it for the stage.[2]

Chekhov believed that our job as actors was to render characters with as much judgment-free detail as possible. And within that attention to each of these tiny facets, lies the beauty we seek to manifest.

Beauty, in the Hindu religion, is an aspect of the divine, which is why Hindu shrines are adorned with artistic paintings and sculptures of the gods and goddesses. Hindus do not believe the pictures themselves are the gods and goddesses, just as photographs of loved ones are not the loved one themselves, but rather are beloved representations of them. Hindus value the divinity inherent in the artist's craft and allow that these beloved representations, whether in paintings, sculptures, song or dance, are the closest portrayals of the poetry of the sacred that are possible to comprehend through the human senses. The divine is made manifest through the artist's loving ability to convey beauty in all its ornate and sacred detail.

In performance we speak about beauty as being that which is striking about the character. Not conventional beauty, but rather the beauty that arrests us, which stops the breath. Beauty can be innocent, youthful, sensual or full. Beauty can also be desperate, horrific, tragic or depraved. There is a beauty in Mary Tyrone's morphine addiction. In Hedda Gabler's cruelty. In the way that Medea loves her children. It is a horrible beauty, but as theatre artists our job is not to place judgment on the sins or the evils of our characters. Rather it is to render the character with deep reverence to the sacred beauty of their story. No matter how abhorrent the truth of that beauty may appear. Only then can we know that which ultimately we may recognize, even to a small degree, within ourselves.

The beautiful face of this kind of divinity often lies deep in the character's vulnerabilities, that which they show only to those they love. Sometimes not even to them or to themselves. That hidden vulnerability often fuels all of the terrible choices the character makes and the performer must pinpoint this vulnerability and reveal it to the audience unflinchingly. Not to condone the character's actions, but to reveal the humanity of the character.

A revelation that seeks to lay bare the source of tragedy, as opposed to merely creating a vehicle for the audience to place blame. Blame is easy. Artists must go further. Artists must seek to discover and share the humanity in every character. It requires bravery. It requires integrity. And in the round, it requires that everything be manifested physically for everyone, everywhere to see.

Exercise 4.1 Avatar

Based on MC's Tool Imaginary Bodies

One of Chekhov's more popular exercises is the Imaginary Body. This exercise allows actors to 'put on' the character's body in order to fully manifest the character onstage:

> You clothe yourself, as it were, with this body. You put it on like a garment. . . . The experience is very similar to that of a real masquerade. And did you ever notice in everyday life how different you feel in different clothes? . . . The imaginary body stands, as it were, between your real body and your psychology, influencing both of them with equal force. Step by step you begin to move, speak and feel in accord with it; that is to say, your character now dwells within you, or if you prefer, you dwell within it.[3]

To allow the performer to fully explore the physicalization of the character, we ask the actor not just to step into the character's shoes, but also into their very skin. They must go beyond the makeup and costume worn onstage to explore what it would mean to live in this other body. In a video game we can become bigger or smaller with a click. When we are acting, we must feel the difference in weight or height. We must let ourselves imagine it. We do that by taking it step by step in creating what Chekhov calls 'The Imaginary Body.' We do it once to introduce the very surface/intellectual ideas an actor has of his/her character. Then we push deeper to let our physical imaginations engage. When the performers stop planning what they should look like and instead begin discovering what has shown up on the body, then the real interesting details begin to emerge.

Coaching Avatar

Based on Chekhov's Imaginary Body Work

Objective: The goal of this exercise is to get the ensemble relaxed and more present in their bodies than in their heads and create character physicalities.

Coach:

- Have actors walk around the room. (Make sure there is enough space to walk, lie down and maybe a few places to sit—whether there are chairs or not. If you have nothing to sit on, the floor will do just fine.)
- Then begin by asking your actors questions:

  - Ask yourself what your character looks like? Are they tall? Short? Fat or thin? How is that different than your body?
  - How would it feel to walk around in their body? Keep going—what does their hair look like, their eyes, their skin? What kind of clothes do they wear? Shoes?
  - Slowly, let your body take on the shape of the body you have in your imagination and when you are ready walk around the room imagining what it feels like to move through space with that body.

- Once they have completed anywhere from 2–5 minutes of this, have them go back to their original spots and stand still with eyes closed.
- Now imagine that picture you just had of the imaginary body of your character. Now imagine that this rendering is a kind of cartoon and you would like a more accurate photograph. Peel back the image in your mind and see the more authentic one underneath. What is the shape of your character's spine? Do they slouch or stand up straight? Do they favor one side to stand on, one hip? What is the expression they hold on their face most of the time. How is their breath? Easy or labored? How does that affect how they move? Begin to see the tiny details that did not show in the first picture. Slowly let yourself move into this new body and begin to walk around the room.

(*continued*)

(continued)

Note: I have sometimes been asked with this exercise what if nothing comes to the actors. The short answer is, if a tool isn't working for an actor—any of the tools—then allow actors to have the freedom to step out and observe everyone else for the duration of the exercise if they like. If the actor doesn't connect with a tool—that's okay. When another tool works later, this one may begin working where it didn't before. In the NMCA pedagogy, they call this phenomenon the 'Christmas light' effect. Some strings of Christmas lights seem not to work when in reality they will work if you find the one bulb to work on. If you find the right bulb and work on just that one light, chances are it will not only work but also light up all the other lights as well. Some tools don't work for some actors right away, and that's fine. But I have also found in exercises like this one that it is important for us as facilitators to trust our actors' imaginations to fill in whatever we ask for, so long as they are not looking to find 'the right answer' or do the exercise in 'the right way.' These thoughts tend to stifle, and if you are worried about this—tell your actors before you begin that there is no right way to do this exercise and no right answer to fall upon. In fact, tell them that if their imagination shows them nothing today, that's okay too. Inspiration and images sometimes need more time to gestate before appearing fully formed. Tell your actors to trust themselves and trust the process.

- Once they have completed anywhere from 2–5 minutes of this, have them go back to their original spots and stand still with eyes closed.
- Now imagine that photograph you just had of the imaginary body of your character. Now imagine that this photograph was sort of airbrushed or photoshopped and that there is an original with more flaws or more flesh. Peel back the image in your mind and see the more authentic one underneath. Begin to manifest this body and when you are ready to open your eyes. As you move through the room, begin to see through this body's eyes, see the people around you—what does this body make of those people? See the space. Feel yourself moving through this group and this place—do you belong here? Yes or no? How

does that change how you move? Try sitting, standing, and when you are ready, engage other people. First just physically and then using sounds. Once you feel comfortable with sounds you can try on the imaginary voice you think matches this body.

Other connections housed within the Avatar exercises are the use of *concentration* and the use of *evolution of image*. Concentration, Chekhov argues, is step one for the actor in training:

The purpose of Concentration seems to be going out of oneself, but really it is going into oneself so deeply that you will find all your abilities trembling and willing to obey. Concentration alone is the door of your own creative ability.[4]

Without a serious concentration on the image of the character, the actor's interpretation of the character falters. Once concentration is achieved, Chekhov encourages the actor to go beyond their initial impression and to dig deeper than initial surface readings: "You, while working on your parts must not think they will come to you fully developed and accomplished. They don't. To complete themselves, to reach a degree of expressiveness that would satisfy you, they will require your active collaboration."[5] Chekhov encourages the use of the evolving image, the idea of peeling the character image back until you see another more accurate/detailed image underneath. The amount of times you can pull back the curtain and find something new is infinite, the determining factor of settling on a character being your own artistic satisfaction. Having a constant well of inspiration to return to can also be useful for performers acting in long runs of a show. The foundation always remains the same, as can the blocking/given circumstances/lines/etc., but 'who shows up' to performance can be a new version every night, keeping the actor engaged as well as her or his partners.

Another exciting way to engage with the image in active collaboration is to allow the character image to have, what Chekhov called, an independent life:

Having caught an image (of a character), look at it and wait until it begins to move, to change, to speak and act on its own. Realize that each image has its own independent life. Don't interfere with this life, but follow it for at least several minutes. Next Step: . . . begin to interfere with it by asking questions or giving orders. "Will you show me how you sit down? Get up? Walk? Ascend or descend a stairway? Meet other people? . . . How do you appear in despair? In a happy mood?"[6]

Working on 'interfering' with the character image in the imagination can lead to wonderful useful discoveries that all come from a place other than the intellect. This interaction can stay in the actor's imagination, influencing choices onstage—but it can also influence physicality if the actor is careful to observe movement and then take the extra step to play with embodying the movements observed.

Exercise 4.2 Time Machine

Based on MC's Tool Back Space/Front Space

In the Chekhov Technique, one of the methods commonly used to affect age and experience is called 'Back Space/Front Space.' The idea is that focusing your energy right outside of your body, either up and out or back and down creates a sense of bringing age and experience with it. This attention and awareness was intricately demonstrated to me in 2006 by Mala Powers, a student of Michael Chekhov's and one of the founders of NMCA. One evening in a master class, she began explaining the idea of back space and front space and allowed herself to show us through demonstration. Previous to this class and throughout the intensive, Mala had been telling us how tired she felt, how run down and that she was finally feeling her age and would have to slow down very soon now. At that time Mala was 74 years old and it was only the very next year that she passed away. But that night, Mala told us she would demonstrate by creating an interpretation of Shakespeare's Juliet by focusing her attention on front space.

She looked down, took some time and after a few moments of deep concentration looked up with a lightness and brightness I can only describe as a happy child full of wonder. The heaviness she had been carrying with her throughout the workshops was gone and in its place was an excitement and a vibrancy. We watched as she spoke to us from that place and in that moment I saw the girl she had once been, and it was extraordinary. This exercise, like so many Chekhov exercises, almost always shows how an actor's focused energy and concentration can palpably and physically translate to an audience. We saw her energy transform. Her focus and concentration clearly showed us someone different before us than the person she had been showing us all week long. It was beyond convincing. It was spooky. It was like some ghost of a girl who died young had taken over Mala's body. We were mesmerized. This exercise allows actors to practice with back space and front space, all the while building their ability to focus and concentrate in such a way that it their energy (and physical character) transforms.

Coaching Time Machine

Based on Chekhov's Back Space/Front Space

Objective: To demonstrate Back Space and Front Space by watching and/or experiencing how the spatial placement of focus and energy can change perception within the audience.

This exercise can be done with one person or as a group. If with one volunteer, choose and then have everyone else sit and watch. If with a group, have half sit out and watch and then let the others sit out and watch. This exercise also invites the actor to imagine the circumstances of their actual life, not their character's life. If working with one actor, ask if the actor is comfortable with thinking about their own life. If they are not, choose another actor and be sure to tell the first actors that using life events is not necessary for the actual tool, only the example and they can watch someone else perform the exercise for the same effect.

Similarly you can have those in the group sit and watch if they prefer. Chekhov was not interested in using actual life events and believed imagination was a better source. So although this exercise doesn't necessarily use actual life event, but rather asks actors to reimagine them, it still may be difficult for some to think about their lives in this way, so allowing them the choice to watch reinforces the kind of safe space necessary for strong vulnerability and risk taking overall. Give actors the choice to sit and watch if performing this exercise is not a good fit for them.

(continued)

(*continued*)

Coach Back Space Time Machine:

- Have each person stand in front of the audience (or imagined audience). Tell them to pull up through their spine, find their IAC and breath. Release any locked knees or tight jaws and breathe. Shoulders down, eyes soft, breathe. Tell them to focus on the breath.
- For NTS, you might have people on all sides, in a circle around the actor. Have the audience note their physicality and their overall energy.
- Then have the actor(s) shut their eyes as they stand in front of the audience and invite them to imagine the circumstances you will give them, letting your words affect them in any way they feel without the need to 'perform.'
- Now ask them to:

  - Imagine yourself a few years from today. Imagine three things that you hoped would happen are happening. The first things that come to your mind are right. Perhaps they have to do with love or courses or career or maybe family. Now imagine something you hoped would not happen is also happening. Perhaps something to do with family or love or health. These things are not insurmountable but they are complicated. And require action and effort on your part. Imagine the memories of how those things came to be building up in the spot right above your shoulder blades but off from your body, weighing down on you.
  - Now imagine five years from that and in this new now, everything has progressed, the complication has gotten better but something new has popped up, perhaps related. Perhaps more difficult. But also some of the positive things in your life have also continued to move forward. Now imagine a big success in your personal life. Imagine the day of that success, despite your other problems. Feel these memories on top of the other memories, like a collage where each image lays over the image that came before. And put all

that energy into your back space, collecting there like more and more seashells washed ashore from the sea.

- Now imagine 10 years from then and your personal life has moved along considerably. Everything you wanted has appeared in someway, but not as you'd anticipate. Why? What things came up that surprised you? That complicated your happiness? That made you turn in a new direction? Perhaps something became exceedingly difficult. And unlivable. Let those memories layer over the others already in that back space.

- Now 10 years from then and your career has suddenly and surprisingly peaked! Your professional life is sensational and exciting, but there is also now a lot of pressure to succeed and your personal life begins to suffer. Greatly. Now imagine your professional life soaring but something in your personal life snaps and will never be the same. Concentrate all your energy on the back space, adding all these new memories to the heap already bearing down on your body and self.

- Now imagine a loss. Something expected but painful. Let those memories mix with all the memories from before. Let the loss color your outlook on the world. Even the successes of your professional life begin to feel heavier.

- Now imagine a new development in your personal life. Something with possibility, something sweet and hopeful. Something in stark contrast to the last few difficult years. Let that new possibility sit atop the pile of memories at the top of a mountain of everything you carry in your back space. Do you trust it? Are you nervous? Are you going to take a chance or is this just too scary? Too much of a risk?

- Now have actors open their eyes, and let the audience just observe their energy, their physicality, what they are sending out to an audience. The difference between when they started

(continued)

(continued)

and where they have arrived should be obvious. Then tell your actors to shake it off and find a new relief in being happily where they are today.

Continue Coaching Front Space Time Machine:

- Now have the same actor, a new actor or the other group who were watching stand and have the first group sit. Then have the actor(s) shut their eyes and just stand in front of the audience (or have the audience in a circle around them), letting your coaching affect them in any way they feel.
- Now ask them to:

  - Imagine a few years ago. Where were you? Imagine that you are there now and that everything that happened since that time was only a dream that you just now woke up from. You are the person you were without any of the successes or troubles that have come your way since then. You wonder what will happen in the next few years, will your life turn out like the dream? Will you make different choices? Put all that wondering and all those corrected mistakes, as well as all those scary possibilities out in front of you, in the space just above your chest—up and out, ballooning away from you, tethered to you by a light string.
  - Now imagine a few years before that. Many of those worries you will have in your future are not here now. Let those future worries and expectations just release from your chest and float up and out to the sky. You are lighter and brighter and less tethered than you were before. And yet there is this restlessness about you. You want to fly up and away like those balloons. But you are strapped down by the feet. Feel the pull up and out and know that someday you will be free to do whatever you want!
  - Now imagine many years before that and you have almost no balloons but only this need to fly! To jump out of your skin and be free. The restlessness consumes you. Focus all that

energy right out and in front of your chest, pulling you up into the big sky. Perhaps the pull makes you nervous. Perhaps the sky is too big. Perhaps you just want to stay close to the warm ground but you are scared you'll just be lifted off and into your life with no control. Feel the pull right out in front of you. There is nothing in the back of you, for better or for worse—there is only the front space, shiny and full of everything awesome that could ever happen but also with huge pockets of doubt and fear of all the ways you could fall. Focus on that space.

• Now have the actors open their eyes, and let the audience just observe their energy, their physicality, what they are sending out to an audience. The difference between when they started, where they got to with back space if they were the ones doing it and where they have arrived should be obvious. Then tell your actors to shake it off and find a new (or returning) relief in being happily where they are today.

Once you have demonstrated back space and front space in this way, ask your actors to begin working with this focused energy with their characters—perhaps during warm-ups daily or just to build the imaginary body.

Exercise 4.3 Project Your Energy

Based on MC's Tool Radiation

Chekhov's focus on receiving and radiating was a large part of his work beyond the radiant Qualities of Movement, not only in the connection between actors, but also in the connections between actors and the audience. Here Wil Kilroy gives actors a chance to engage in their own energetic ability to radiate out in multiple directions, instead of the merely 'cheating out' style of energy-sharing we are commonly accustomed to.

Actors engaged in a 'Project Your Energy' exercise.
Credit: Gordon Wenzel

Coaching Project Your Energy

Based on Chekhov's Ideas of Radiation

By Wil Kilroy

Objective: To physically experience radiating your acting energy in all directions, increasing your ability to fill a space completely

Coach:

- While directions and footwork could vary, the concept of sending out energy remains the same, even if the outward mechanics are altered. However, here is one specific version, which is adapted from Michael Chekhov's legato/staccato exercise.
- Actors begin by spreading around the room, being sure they have space all around them. They stand in what is commonly known as 'neutral' but perhaps we call center: 'relaxed with an engaged IAC' and with the spine in alignment and hands dropped by their sides.
- Now ask the actors to fully engage their imaginations as they lunge forward on their right foot, being sure to keep their torso erect, and extending their arms forward with energy flowing through each fingertip. As they maintain this pose, encourage them to send energy from their kneecaps, from their toes, from their heart, and via the eyes—without tension but instead with a sense of ease via the engaged imagination. After a few moments of sending the energy forward from every cell of the body, step back to center.

Actors engaged in a 'Project Your Energy' exercise.

Credit: Gordon Wenzel

Note from Anjalee: This exercise requires some 'tension.' Obviously not anything painful or uncomfortable, but a sense of resistance. Without it, the radiation will not be as effective. If you find actors only 'sort of' doing the exercise, remind them that they will get out of it only so much as they put in. For the first few rounds try to do this exercise with them to demonstrate this needed tension; position yourself in front of the room so they can follow you without trying to remember what comes next. Coming back to center in between each move allows for a release of tension after every movement.

- Next lunge with the right foot, arms extending over to the right. Again, send energy from every part of the body over to the right, always being sure that the eyes are alive and engaged. Return to center.
- Next, lunge over to the left and radiate the energy. Back to center. Next step back with the left foot and press the palms of the hands behind you, still with an erect torso, and send all of your energy and awareness into that space. Project energy through your entire back, through the hips, through the calves, through your heels. The eyes are still active but it's as if they are focused on feeling the energy behind them. Return to center.
- Next, step just slightly forward with the right foot and point the fingertips down toward the ground. Imagine sending all of your

(continued)

(*continued*)

energy underneath you in order to feel grounded and supported. Return to center.

- Now take a slight step forward with the left foot and extend your fingertips up to the sky. Imagine your energy extending through the roof of the building and up to the heavens. Return to center. You can continue this slowly or quickly, depending on what is needed at the moment—slowly to gain focus and stability or quickly in order to generate a whirlwind of energy as might be needed for a specific character or scene. As previously mentioned, the exact foot placement isn't essential, but the pattern explained above is right, right, left, left, right left. Then you are ready to repeat with the right foot again for another round.

Note: As an addition to Wil's wonderful exercise, I like to have actors move through the above rotation twice slow (or legato), twice fast (or staccato) and then end with either just the breath and the imagination (imagining sending energy forward, center, right, center, left, center, down, center, up, center) or just the imagination alone. You can call out the words if the actors are new to the exercise both when you are doing it physically and in the internal version. Eventually you will not need to call anything out, they will remember. As an internal movement, lovely magic can happen with your actors' ability to hold the stage in silence when they practice this kind of projection often.

Actors engaged in 'Project Your Energy from Within' exercise.
Credit: Gordon Wenzel

Exercise 4.4 Filling Space: The Full Body Dance

Based on MC's Tools Expansion and Radiation

In Chekhov's *Lessons for the Professional Actor,* he talks about the importance of Expansion through Radiation: "Now let us look at our method. Everything in it has the tendency to break the boundaries of our bodies, our voices . . . Or let us look at radiation, which means to give out everything I have inside."[7] Here Wil Kilroy uses music, similar to Exercise 3.2 'Elemental Physicality with Music' in Chapter 3, but in this exercise the use of music encourages the actor to 'give out everything he has inside' with specific awareness of the 360 degree nature of both the body and the body in the space. An excellent follow up to Exercise 4.3 'Project Your Energy,' 'Filling the Space' is a strong way to get actors used to using all sides of their body to express their characters. When working on a specific production, be sure to choose music that creates atmospheres within the play and/or music that encourages expression of specific characters or relationships. This could also be a great warm-up for a production, putting them in the world of the play through music while also reminding them to send out their energy in all directions, not just pushed forward.

Coaching the Full Body Dance

Based on Chekhov's Ideas of Expansion and Radiation

By Wil Kilroy

Objective: For actors to realize that their movement choices are limitless, and that it's natural to extend themselves in all directions when they are fully expressive.

Coach:

- Actors spread about the room, being sure to have space around them and with no need to observe each other at the start, but instead to remain in their own 'world.'
- Music is then started, and depending on what outcome is needed for a particular project, it might be upbeat or more lyrical.

(continued)

(*continued*)

This exercise should follow a basic physical warm-up so that actors are already loose and ready to be physically creative.

- Actors are now instructed to move just their head and neck in conjunction with the music—the rest of the body remaining still. They can move with the beat, at half time or even double time, but always being aware of the music and continuously changing their movement.

- Encourage the actors to move the head and neck in a variety of ways. What can you do with just the head and neck? You can drop from side to side, you can jut the head forward and back, you can roll.

- Actors are coached to not move in what might be a habitual way to music, but instead to consider this as creative movement and attempt to find the most variety possible in moving the head and neck.

- Next the head and neck becomes still and the shoulders are isolated and begin to move—in unison, independently, up, down, circling and lifting.

- Next, only the torso moves, which can be just the rib cage forward and back or side to side or in a circle, or the entire torso bending forward or side to side.

- Next it's just the hips circling, shaking side to side or front to back, thrusting and lifting at all different tempos.

- Next it's only the feet moving. What can these amazing feet do? They can jump, they can slide, they can point in and point out, the heels can lift, and the toes can lift.

- After isolating and moving these different parts of the body, now return to just the head and neck, then add the shoulders, add the torso, add the arms/hands/fingers, add the hips and add the feet—now the whole body will be engaged.

- Again, be sure to coach the actors to keep exploring and not to fall into their typical way of dancing.

- Call out low, high, left, right, back, front—so that the actors are expressing physically in all directions.

- Once all the actors are moving creatively in all directions, you might call out images for them to portray such as be a wave, a dolphin, or just pure joy.
- You might also call out one actor for everyone to mirror—not following every move precisely but instead trying to mirror the essence of energy being expressed. Actors can also work in pairs, working to sync their movement without either of them leading, but instead staying in the present moment and improvising.

Exercise 4.5 Bring Them In

Based on MC's Ideas on Receiving

An excellent complementary exercise to the 'Full Body Dance' would be what I call 'Bring Them In.'

Coaching Bring Them In

Based on MC's Ideas on Receiving

Objective: To invite the audience into the space and play through movement.

In this exercise, we receive the audience actively, which Chekhov describes as 'drawing in': "As to how the receiving should be executed and felt, the actor must bear in mind that it is more than a matter of merely looking and listening onstage. To actually receive means to draw towards one's self with the utmost inner power of things, persons or events of the situation."[8]

Coach:

- Run the whole 'Full Body Dance' exercise above.
- Next, return to the same music, either on the same day or a subsequent day, but this time ask actors to draw the audience in from every direction, draw the audience toward them.

(continued)

(*continued*)

- Other variations would be to let half the cast radiate and the other half receive, or to let half the group watch while the other half radiates and receives and then discuss the differences.
- Another exciting variation that could prepare the actors for an opening is to let the actors in the audience radiate while the actors onstage receive and vice versa. This attention to the energy passed back and forth through the audience and onto the stage may very well over time result in the keen sensitivity in your actors' ability to read the audience and adjust their performance based on what the audience needs and wants.

Exercise 4.6 Expanding from the Self into Outer Space

Based on MC's Tool Focal Points

Michael Chekhov, Konstantin Stanislavski as well as many modern-day practitioners like Patsy Rodenburg have often touted the exciting use of the tool known as 'Focal Points.' An excellent way for actors to break up the 'locked-in' feeling of a scene in which two actors unnaturally stare at each other during the length of a scene, this technique offers a more natural variety and a method for physically scoring the gaze during a scene. Patsy Rodenburg's '3 Circles of Presence' and Stanislavski's 'Circles of Attention' focus on three distinct circles. The Chekhov Technique utilizes five.

Actors engaged in a 'Focal Points' exercise.
Credit: Gordon Wenzel

Coaching Focal Points

Based on Chekhov's Ideas of Expansion and Imaginary Body

By Wil Kilroy

Objective: With this exercise actors become aware that they have a variety of places where they can focus their attention and particularly their eyes during a scene. Particularly new actors often feel obligated to stare into one another's eyes while delivering dialogue, which is not realistic. This exercise will open up a variety of choices as to eye 'life' (what is going on with regards to eye movement within each moment on stage).

Coach the Introduction to Focal Points:

- Actors can 'play themselves' for this set of exercises, meaning they don't have to create a character. They are just exploring their own experiences of the focal points.
- Working in teams, actors begin an improvisational dialogue but they are going to be focused directly on their physical self— perhaps rubbing at a stain on their shirt or playing with a button. This will be Focal Point #1.
- Next the actors continue their conversation but now look directly at each other, which is Focal Point #2.
- Continuing the same conversation, each actor now looks around the environment, being sure to really look and take note of the space. This is Focal Point #3.
- Next the actors bring their focus up within their mind—recalling a memory, or a task they need to accomplish later—taking them away from the present moment although they continue dialoguing with their partner from this state, which is Focal Point #4.
- Next the actors 'space out' for a moment, so that their focus is nowhere, or perhaps everywhere, maybe connecting with an ethereal presence, while still carrying on a dialogue. None of us maintains this state for long, but moments of it can be quite effective in certain situations and it is Focal Point #5.

(continued)

(continued)

Actors engaged in a 'Focal Points' exercise.
Credit: Gordon Wenzel

Coach the Imaginary Body Improv:

- For this set of exercises, we bring in the characters that actors might be working on.
- Once the actor is inhabiting their character's imaginary body via one of the springboard tools provided in other exercises in this book (try 4.1 Avatar), allow them to walk in the space as their character while you guide them with open statements.
- First the actors repeat "My name is . . ." and spontaneously fill in the blank. Always remind the actors that there is no right or wrong to this work and to simply go with whatever first enters their head.
- The actors then continuously repeat this line, stating their name, until you move onto another open statement such as "I love. . . ." or "I hate . . ."
- After a few of these statements, the actors then gather in a circle and one by one go around and reveal, remaining in character, the statements they completed.
- Once everyone has taken a turn, the 'characters' are then asked to go find another character that they related to, or want something from, and improvisation begins. These can be in pairs or groups of three or four. Actors are then asked to experiment with the different focal points, moving through each one at some point in the improv.
- All the actors can then be asked to freeze, and you can tap one grouping at a time in order to 'listen in' on what is transpiring.
- Once this is complete you can have two actors run an improvisation while two other actors (one assigned to each improvisor) randomly call out focal points for them.

Exercise 4.7 Getting it off Our Chest: Freeing the Tension in the Chest, Shoulders, Neck and Jaw

Inspired by MC's Ideas on Sensations/Falling

Continuing our work into sensations, Samantha Norton uses an exercise that focuses on the breath, voice and the authentic place of the 'fall' to release tension. This release allows for a deeper full body resonance from all sides of the body.

Coaching Getting it off Our Chest

Inspired by MC's Ideas on Sensations/Falling

By Samantha Norton

Objective: An exercise to release unnecessary tension from the shoulders and jaw.

Thanks to our technological devices, our heads and neck are spending quite a bit of time jutted forward, which creates extra tension from the shoulders up into the jaw. 'Shake it off' is a partner exercise that offers a wonderful muscular release while opening up the vocal range.

Coach:

• To begin, have your students partner with someone at a similar height. Student (A) takes a grounded stance while placing their hands on the pectoral (chest) muscles, just below the collarbone of student (B). Student (B) leans fully into the hands of Student (A). Trusting their partner to keep them from falling, student (B) vocalizes any sound that comes out while student (A) shakes (B).

• After each partner has had a go, have your students try the shaking exercise on the back. This mini-massage releases shoulder tension and feels great.

• The next fun step requires a bit more trust but the results can be extremely insightful and freeing. Partner (B) allows their full weight to be held by (A). When (A) is ready, they replace shaking their partner with a small release and catch of (B). Partner (B) vocalizes at the point of 'falling' into the hands of (A). Imagine the sound you make while swooping down on a roller coaster.

(continued)

(*continued*)

The fall and catch exercise gives the students a visceral feeling of the high, wide and free sounds their voices can make without tension. For me, this exercise is more effective than the traditional 'siren' exercise because our brains are preoccupied with the activity and not trying to 'get it right.'

Note from Anjalee: When actors are doing this exercise, remind them to be mindful of their own body. If anything feels painful or uncomfortable, they should stop the exercise. Overall, although the exercise can feel strange, it should also feel good. Also, as a facilitator be mindful of actors' necks as they work through this exercise. Have actors drop their heads forwards when they have partners allowing them to 'fall back.' This will protect the neck from too much flopping around.

Advice from the Pros: Lighting in Non-Proscenium Spaces

By Heath Hansum

Theatre in the round, end stage, alley and some thrust stage configurations are examples of non-proscenium spaces and many of these theatres also have a reduced size in common. Small spaces present excellent opportunities for the audience to really be part of the mood and action of the performance. In this essay, I will focus primarily on pragmatic design and some technical considerations in small spaces. Hard and fast rules, however, will be nearly non-existent because, as we know in theatre, there is no one right answer.

A Problem with Intimacy

Creating an effective intimate environment can be a challenge in live performance, at least for the designers. What is a close personal interaction for one audience member is seen from a completely different perspective to another. What does intimacy accomplish for the production? Certainly it depends on the audience member. Some like

Heath Hansum, sound and lighting designer, technical coordinator, Bucknell University.

Credit: Heath Hansum

to be 'up close and personal' with the performers and environment while many like the relative safety of being on the other side of the fourth wall. As a person who has designed and built focusing on the near field for a variety of productions, I will say it's a good idea to have a firm sense of your prospective audience before selecting a performance style. Seasoned theatre patrons may find a traditional proscenium arrangement, where there is 20 feet or more of viewing distance to the stage, boring. They would much rather the invigorating experience of sharing the space and hearing the between line breaths of the performer. Perhaps the choice of performance space will not be up to you but choosing to be in a non-proscenium venue raises some important issues.

How Will You Tell the Story?

Each designer has to think about the challenges of creating the world of the play in this unique space. What type of scenery might be required to help tell the visual story of the production? The practicality of seeing over or around scenery is important to consider when determining size and style of performance space. When we think of proscenium spaces we often think of rolling wagons or wing-and-drop style scenery but these are used less often in non-traditional spaces. Scenery is often smaller and more stylized. Simple but symbolic set dressing or props are popular choices as they serve as elemental suggestions of time and period. Costumes and properties are viewed from a much closer vantage, so if they want to appear real, more detail may needed to be added.

Related to scenery and the focus of this essay is lighting. What might be required? Often directors and some designers don't think of lighting beyond 'I need to see the actor.' Even basic illumination is occasionally a challenge when the performance area breaks the barrier into the audience. Many theatre patrons are used to seeing a play similar to seeing a movie in a theatre, sitting comfortably in the dark looking at a lighted picture. In round, alley and even thrust stages, we are often very close to or even *in* that lit space.

It's All about the Angles

As a lighting designer, one of my challenges is to find the delicate balance of appropriately lighting the performers in all the areas of blocking while creating a pleasant and appropriate viewing experience for the audience. Few people enjoy bright theatre lights in their face while trying to invest in a production. How can you avoid this problem? In short, sometimes you simply can't. Often there is just so much overlap between performance and audience space that you find yourself lighting the patrons. If that's the case, try to keep your angles relatively steep and if possible use more light sources so you are able to keep the intensity as low as possible. If you are able, consider reducing the number of changes 'cues,' as fluctuating light levels can often be more distracting than a consistent degree of illumination. It's worthwhile to take a second look at the geometry here and make sure you can make the shot without lighting up unwanted areas. Prudent attention to where the light fixture is placed is important. Using shutters (or lens accessories) allows you the option to more effectively slice the acting area away from the house. A steeper lighting angle can make all the difference. An early discussion with the costume designer as to the headwear (hat brim shadows especially) is a great idea. If shallower lighting angles are desired, perhaps blocking can be adjusted minimally to avoid making audience members squint.

Shooting beyond the Target

A major consideration in lighting involves what I call 'waste light.' That is the light that continues past your intended target. Is this only a consideration in small close quarters? Certainly not, but it's so much easier to deal with light splashing off into the wing behind a masking leg than into an audience member's lap who is seated six feet away. I've always thought that I could get very rich if I could invent a light that I could set to be bright for only a certain distance and then go dark.

Close quarters stage lighting.
Credit: Heath Hansum

As soon as such a light reached the torso of the actor, it would immediately fall off in intensity. Alas, this is only available in some computer-aided rendering programs and doesn't represent real life. The waste light can be troublesome, especially in a close full-round stage set up. You should discuss and decide if you want a similar-looking stage picture from all sides or are you creating a performance that is unique to every seat and perhaps patrons are encouraged to come back another night for another view. I've heard audience members say "Good show. I bet it's interesting from the other side." Most non-traditional space directors and designers will make a habit of watching rehearsals from new places in the house as often as possible to get the feel of the show from all angles.

Quiet Please

What is noisy about lighting? Twenty-five years ago, there may have been little to nothing in the space making unwanted sounds during a show but times have changed. Many modern light fixtures and accessories have small fans built in to keep them cool. Some moving lights can make noise when they are repositioning or making an internal change. If a data projector is used for video or slides, then fans will almost certainly be part of the environment. These little devices are of little consequence when they are 30 or more feet away from your patrons but in small round or thrust theatres they may be hanging just a few feet above heads and at that distance it doesn't take much to become distracting. What is to be done? Many fixtures have modes that include a 'quiet' mode for just this scenario. If using moving lights, the cue times that control the moves can be slowed to quiet the fixture or timed with an event on stage that will pull focus.

Most all productions need a stage manager of some sort coordinating events and calling cues for the various running crewmembers of the production. Often in small theatres, there isn't a proper booth for people whose job is to talk during the production. It stands to reason that she or he needs to see and hear the events on stage to perform their duties and we don't want the audience hearing "standby light cue thirty" before a cue. Talking very quietly and positioning the headset mic close to the mouth may solve it. More likely, some sort of physical barrier should be considered. Remote locations that don't have a window with a direct sight line may require one or more closed circuit cameras to be the eyes in the space and a microphone for the ears. Stage managers and lights can be just one of a handful of unwanted noises in your performance space. Don't get me started on heating and air conditioning systems. This was supposed to be about lighting.

Wrapping up the Package

The production is a kind of gift that you have worked hard to prepare for your audience and just as you do when you want to impress a beloved family member, you make sure the corners are folded nicely and the

Radium Girls by D.W. Gregory. In the round production directed by Anjalee Deshpande Hutchinson, lighting design by Heath Hansum, costume design by Jenny Kenyon, scenic design by F. Elaine Williams. Bucknell University 2015.

Credit: Mark Hutchinson

ribbons have the right amount of curl. Small spaces will be an opportunity to arrange details. The director can work with the actors to deliver the critical facial expression that wouldn't be seen in a big theatre. The scenic designer can utilize a fine paint technique for that ideal faux marble floor and the lighting designer will shape this world with gentle light distribution that helps tell the story and allows the audience to enjoy the nuances in this private little space.

Notes

1 Michael Chekhov, *On the Technique of Acting*. New York: Harper, 1993, p. 18.
2 Michael Chekhov, *To the Actor: On the Technique of Acting*. London: Routledge, 2002, p. 90.
3 Chekhov, *To the Actor*, p. 79.
4 Michael Chekhov, *Lessons for Teachers of His Acting Technique*. Ottawa: Dovehouse Editions, 2000, p. 42.
5 Chekhov, *To the Actor*, p. 23.
6 Chekhov, *To the Actor*, p. 29.
7 Chekhov, *Lessons for Teachers*, p. 141.
8 Chekhov, *To the Actor*, p. 19.

Blood Wedding by Federico Garcia Lorca, adapted by Caridad Svich. Alley production directed by Anjalee Deshpande Hutchinson, lighting design by Heath Hansum, set design by F. Elaine Williams, costume design by Jenny Kenyon. Bucknell University 2009.

Credit: Enche Tjin

Credit: drawing courtesy of Pablo Guerra-Monje

5

CRAFTING THE RHYTHM
OF TRUTH

There is a paradox in performing in a non-traditionally staged piece and it has everything to do with movement. In order for each person in the audience of an NTS in-the-round production to get the best possible view of the piece, actors must constantly be in motion. They must continue to move throughout beats, transitions, etc. If they do not, audiences are stuck with only one viewpoint of the play. Even worse, at any given point, someone in the audience can't see the faces of the actors. Maybe they are sitting in a seat that favors the unfortunate angle in which two people are blocking each other so that all the audience member gets is one back. If this is happening throughout the play, audiences give up and disengage, so actors must commit to constantly moving so that each and every audience member gets to see the best possible performance from their exact angle and location in the house.

Similarly, when working on the thrust stage, actors must move in consideration of the audience on all three sides, sometimes working as if in the round (downstage), sometimes working as if on a proscenium (upstage). Alley requires that the movement considers two different shows on both sides of the audience and giving each audience the attention they deserve, in addition to catering to an unusually wide length of performance space. With site specific, movement is the key to a tailored experience. The audience must be considered in tandem with the space. Even if the space is beautifully designed and the performance is beautifully rendered, one must always consider the audience experience—and consider how to make that experience manifest for everyone in the audience, not just the selected or lucky few.

The paradox of the NTS piece lies in the fact that even though this kind of movement can feel very unrealistic to the actor, it can actually feel more realistic to an audience, in comparison to performances created for the proscenium stage. To an audience, the typical 'turning out to the fourth wall' associated with proscenium (and thrust to some degree), can feel unrealistic, but the audience allows for it with their suspension of disbelief if it is done well. In an arena staging, the audience doesn't see actors favoring any one side or 'turning out.' They see actors engaged in a more true to life physical dynamic, and in this way, the audience's sense of what they are watching becomes more intimate, more like an insider to the action on the stage rather than an observer. (This is magnified in site-specific work.) This can only happen successfully if the action is supported and justified well. Otherwise the movement can feel exhausting or like an elaborate artificial dance.

The key to a well-supported physical score onstage then becomes half about the director choosing what to show when and to whom, and half about the actor being very clear about the physical choices they make onstage from the beginning to middle to the end. It is true that this kind of specificity of choice is important for any kind of theatre, but in NTS performance it is not only important, it is crucial. Without being very intentional about what we show to whom and when as performers and directors, we don't make a less than perfect gift—we fail to share the gift to many in the audience, at all.

Exercise 5.1 Managing Mind Sweat

Inspired by MC's Ideas on Feeling of Ease

Konstantin Stanislavski constantly maintained that tension was the enemy. That it was the 'Occupational Hazard' of the actor: "Muscular tautness interferes with inner emotional experience."[1] Both Stanislavski and Chekhov believed that those engaged in powerful performances did not have the interference of actor tension.

However, some actors argue that some tension in necessary. Great ballet dancers must appear relaxed when actually there is a fine muscular tension that allows them to do their work. Michael Chekhov's answer to this paradox was to seek out exercises that encouraged a feeling of 'ease' rather than relaxation. He describes ease as that which "Relaxes your body and spirit, therefore it is also much akin to humor."[2] A person at ease may have some tension, the tension it requires to sit up or to walk about, yet they also have a lightness to their movements that is palpable to anyone watching them.

A feeling of ease requires a kind of clarity in the performance. Clarity in performance begins with clarity with the performer. One good way to begin rehearsal is to begin with a practice of clearing the day away so that the performers can focus their attention and concentration completely on the piece. Meditation can be a good palate cleanser for the mind. A Zen master named Ed once told me that meditating does not mean silencing the mind completely. In fact silencing the mind is next to impossible for most people. Meditation is more about slowing the mind, helping it to move on from its fixations, being directly accountable for one's attention and what it fixates or focuses on. But thoughts will come regardless of our work to keep them away. The master said, "The mind produces thought like the body produces sweat. It is a normal function of a healthy mind."

Our job then becomes not to keep the mind from 'sweating' but rather to allow the mind to wash the sweat away periodically. This is easier said than done and there is no one on earth that is perfect at this task. Okay maybe the Dalai Lama. For the rest of us, it is a practice of mindfulness, but in this case practice will never make perfect. Being perfect at meditating is not the goal of meditating. Just as perfecting how to shower is not the goal of showering. Getting clean and perhaps also relaxing is the goal of showering. Clearing the mind and relaxing is the goal of meditation. It doesn't matter how good you are at showering, the act of taking the shower completes the goal.

Meditation is one tool that can help an actor focus on the present moment by helping her/him release some of the other moments the mind is fixated on in order to find the actor's natural starting point. It can act as a reboot to the attention. Focusing on the present moment is one of the most vital components of creating the dynamic needed for the engaged performance. It also allows one to release unnecessary tension in the physicality and encourages a feeling of ease. This feeling of ease can allow for a kind of receptivity that tension sometimes blocks. This receptivity, which Chekhov calls the ability to 'Receive,' allows actors to react in the moment to their partners, keeping their performances both emotionally and kinesthetically dynamic. In addition, it also allows actors to stay open to audience energy and response, which heightens the experience of the performance for everyone.

Coaching Mind Sweat

Connected to Chekhov's Ideas on Feeling of Ease

Objective: To release unnecessary tension and open up a deeper sense of receptivity from the actor.

Coach the Preparation:

- Have each actor find a comfortable place to sit on the floor. They can sit cross-legged or sit on their ankles in a low kneel. Pillows can be used as a cushion. Actors can also use chairs if desired, and a folded hand towel under the tailbone can help with alignment here.
- Ask actors not to slouch but also not to sit up ramrod straight. Ask them to find the comfortable place where the spine is aligned. If this is confusing, have them slouch and then sit up very straight and then find the comfortable place in between. Or have them lean against a wall with a pillow or towel underneath their tailbone in a place that is comfortable, tipping slightly forward.
- Once they have found this place, ask them to remember it, this is their 'Zazen' (literally 'Seated Meditation' in Zen Buddhism) position for today.

Coach the Gentle Release:

- Next have them lay down. Once the actors are lying down, have them uncross anything (arms, legs, etc.) and use the pillows or towels to cushion anything that is uncomfortable. If they want, they can raise their knees up with their feet resting flat on the floor. The goal is that they are at a place of release with the least amount of physical 'holding' (holding their arms crossed, holding an expression, holding their belly in, etc.).

- Then begin to coach a relaxation or visualization exercise. Here is one example, coach (slowly):

  - Take a nice deep breath in. Then release. Another deep cleansing breath in, and release. One final breath in and release.
  - Beginning with your toes, begin to bring your attention and awareness down to your feet. What is going on with your feet today? Any pain? Any tension? Any tightness? Focus on your feet from your toes through your arches up to your heel and then ankles and comb through for any tightness or pain.
  - If you find any, use the breath to focus on that area, then take a nice breath in and exhale, allowing the tension in your foot to gently give a little (or a lot) with the release of breath.

- Follow this pattern of attention, breath and release all the way up the actor's bodies, from calves to thighs all the way up to the top of the head. Do not skip the groin and buttocks! They may giggle (if they are a younger ensemble) at first but it is essential that they release tension even in this part of the body.
- Once you have finished with the top of the head, have them scan their body one more time looking for any residual tension or stress. Where do they hold it personally? Have them focus more breath there and release.
- Guide actors to let release happen naturally. There is no 'right' or 'wrong' way to do this—just as there is no right or wrong way to fall asleep. Tell them just the intention of asking the body to release is sometimes enough and to use the breath to help them.
- End with final big breath for the whole body, and then ask them to come to their Zazen position. When they come to that position, tell them they can close their eyes or leave them half open in soft focus (not really looking at anything, but looking past a fixed point in space).

(continued)

(continued)

Coach the Breath Work (a pause is a beat, or about 2–4 seconds—feel out what is right for you):

- Once they are all there, ask them to breathe as you direct and coach:

    - Breathe in (count) 2, 3, 4—pause
    - Breathe out 2, 3, 4—pause
    - Breathe in 2, 3, 4, 5—pause
    - Breathe out 2, 3, 4, 5—pause
    - Breathe in 2, 3, 4, 5, 6—pause
    - Breathe out 2, 3, 4, 5, 6—pause
    - Breathe in 2, 3, 4, 5, 6, 7—pause
    - Breathe out 2, 3, 4, 5, 6, 7—pause
    - Going down (numbers)
    - Breathe in (count) 2, 3, 4, 5, 6—pause
    - Breathe out 2, 3, 4, 5, 6—pause
    - Breathe in 2, 3, 4, 5—pause
    - Breathe out 2, 3, 4, 5—pause
    - Breathe in 2, 3, 4—pause
    - Breathe out 2, 3, 4—pause.

Note: You can choose to guide them to try to situate the breath deep in the belly (diaphragm) and/or full in the chest (as is often the protocol in acting exercises to increase breath control for lines) but I find that for meditation exercises, allowing for a more shallow breath can sometimes bring greater depth of awareness to younger actors or those unfamiliar with meditation. Either way is ultimately fine but shallow breath may allow the novice actor to focus more on release than perfecting form.

However, for a more trained actor, suggesting a more full but constricted from the throat breath, such as the Hatha Yoga 'Ujjayi' breath (otherwise known as the Ocean Breath) may keep the advanced actor more grounded in the physical practice of the meditation exercise while also concentrated on a deeper more full focus on diaphragmatic breath and breath control. This variation is a choice.

No matter what you choose, remind actors to be conscious of what is personally comfortable at any given time and to let go of the need to follow your lead or 'perfect' the breaths if it is no longer comfortable or they feel light headed. Give them the permission 'to leave the path provided and return to it at will.'

Coach the Thought Observation:

- Now tell them to take a big breath in and release. Then follow this breath with some breaths that are slow and deep. Allow them to relax and let their breathing fall to whatever is comfortable for them. Perhaps shallow or perhaps deep. Tell them to try to take four counts to breathe in, wait two beats and then take six counts for the exhale.
- Wait one beat and begin again. Ask them to focus their attention and awareness on the breath. When thoughts come in, allow them to happen, observe them and then return the attention to the breath. One image I often give is to have people imagine their thoughts as clouds drifting across and then out of the blue sky above them.
- Another image is connecting the breath to a walk in the woods, and each thought as something encountered along the way— an interesting flower, a dead raccoon, a ripe berry bush, an old cigarette butt. One can feel free to look at the object, but one must move on, which for us would be returning our attention to the counted breath rather than whatever has turned our head. Sometimes we may find ourselves carrying the dead raccoon with us. Sometimes for miles on our walk. It seems to just keep appearing but it is really we who are carrying it. This is natural and can happen at stressful points in our lives. Encourage your actors not to beat themselves up about it but just to acknowledge this is something that they are dealing with. Encourage your actors to 'observe' rather than 'judge' what is going on. If we go back to our shower metaphor—this is the dye stain on your fingers that may take a few showers to fully remove. Or perhaps it is a wound that will heal into a scar, which you will

(continued)

(*continued*)

> always feel when you shower, but will eventually stop bleeding with time. Clean your emotional wounds by allowing your attention to move on from them for longer and longer periods.

Meditation before a rehearsal, from the relaxation/visualization through the Zazen should take anywhere from 10 to 15 minutes. This is excellent preparation for concentration exercises.

A Note on Fatigue

Both Michael Chekhov and Konstantin Stanislavski were a bit wary regarding meditation, particularly laying down meditation. Although they were both big proponents of letting go of muscle tension as an essential tool that relates to peak performance onstage (character tension is exciting to watch, actor tension is embarrassing to watch), both also saw the potential in meditation to lead to lethargy. I find this is true if actors are in a state of chronic fatigue. College/high school students who spend a lot of time focusing on social life, schoolwork, extracurricular engagements, in rehearsal, etc. are often prime candidates for chronic fatigue. This is usually exacerbated if the students don't engage in strong self-care routines, making healthy choices in sleeping, eating and exercising well.

If you find that some of your ensemble leans into lethargy or outright falls asleep during meditation, ask them to sit up and lean against the wall as described earlier in their 'Zazen' position. This position can often give them the benefits of a meditation session without falling into the temptation of outright sleep. Tell students to monitor themselves, and if they are falling asleep, if they are very tired or if they have just 'pulled an all-nighter,' to begin and end meditation in the Zazen position. They can even shift into the Zazen position at any point during their meditation if they feel their energy transitioning into sleep mode. In the Zen tradition, meditation is not used as a method to relax but as a way to 'Wake Up' the energy and attention within. This tool can be used in that way as well. You can also use any part of the tool (body relaxation, counted breath, silent meditation) on its own if that suits your ensemble better. The goal is to take a mental shower and reboot the system so that actors are ready to focus on your next task (whatever that may be) completely. Encourage meditation that is an active rather than passive activity!

Lastly, if any of your actors come out still feeling tension rather than lethargy, let them know that it is okay—that sometimes all they need to do is imagine what it would feel like to be relaxed and let their body show that relaxation on the outside. Often 'manually' putting the body in a place of relaxation either kick starts the internal process and/ or creates the clean slate for the audience no matter what is going on underneath. This 'clean slate' of relaxation is what Chekhov refers to as 'A Feeling of Ease.' A feeling of ease doesn't mean that you are necessarily at ease, it means that you are showing a feeling of ease to the audience. What you are feeling underneath can be something different altogether.

A Note on Feeling

What an actor feels is not necessarily what an audience feels. An actor creates an experience for the audience, that doesn't mean the actor has to feel what the audience is feeling. Ever heard the phrase "If you let the character cry, the audience won't." Craftsmanship of performance is often highly underrated but integral to the performer, especially for performers with lengthy careers or those in long runs. You cannot always 'feel' the experience of your character. It is emotionally impossible. Chekhov suggests instead of trying to 'feel' it, create the shape of it. The shape of crying— how do you cry with your hands, your back, your breath? What is the shape of laughing? The shape of ease? When inspiration fails (as it is bound to do sometimes) that is when you need technique.

Using tools to feel sensations (the sensation of falling) instead of emotion (the feeling of regret) or tools to use image (a dandelion releasing seeds to the wind) instead of ideas (let go of all my tension now!), actors can sometimes connect more clearly to what they are trying to create for an audience, rather than trying to experience something for the audience.

Exercise 5.2 Walking Meditation
Inspired by MC's Ideas on Feeling of Ease

The walking meditation is a variation on the Zazen 'Mind Sweat' exercise, and it can be used in addition and/or on its own. In this exercise, we once again work to detach from what the mind is fixating on and instead focus on breath as a way to reboot the system and start from a place of neutral. In addition to the breath, in walking meditation we also add movement. The movement of the foot. And then the other foot. The hope is that you clear the mind and relax but also that you get into a place of flow.

Flow is the place where your focus on the task at hand changes your perception of being. Your awareness of self and of time shifts. Walking meditation can take you from a place of fretting about the minutiae of your life to feeling yourself pull right up into the present. Once you shift your attention to the present moment, you will find the work in rehearsal (or performance) becomes much stronger. You become able to really listen to your partner, and therefore react

Actors engaged in Walking Meditation.
Credit: Gordon Wenzel

in a more spontaneous and authentic manner. You worry less about pleasing and focus more on being. You find yourself leaning into the audience experience and building on it rather than worrying about it. You find yourself more able to pursue the objective of your character in such a way that at the end of the scene/act/play, you don't even really remember the 'performance' of it because you were so deeply committed to the intention of the character. Walking meditation is one way of preparing you to get there.

Coaching Walking Meditation

Connected to Chekhov's Ideas on Feeling of Ease

Objective: To release unnecessary tension and open up a deeper sense of receptivity from the actor.

Coach the Walking Meditation 1:

- If possible, ask actors to take off their shoes and socks for this exercise. If it is not possible, then just socks is better than full on with shoes. The sensation of the foot actually touching the floor makes this exercise in concentration more viscerally engaging. Make sure to have a clean swept space to begin.
- If you are using this exercise at the beginning of a rehearsal, ask your actors to just move around the room at their normal pace just taking stock of their bodies and their energy levels.
- If you are using this exercise at the end of a rehearsal, make sure to have an energetic exercise to precede this one and when that one finishes, ask your actors to just move around the room at their normal pace taking stock of their bodies and their energy levels.

Note: This constant check in helps train actors to know when they need to bring their energy up or bring it in for performance by knowing where they are at to begin with—the first step is train for a kind of personal observation and regular energetic 'inventory.'

(*continued*)

(*continued*)

- When ready, ask your actors to begin to slow down, still allowing their bodies to move as if they are walking at a normal pace. Let the movement gradually become 'slow motion' around the room.

- Once they are there, ask them to begin to shift their focus to their breath and feet. Starting with the breath, inhale on the count of five; exhale on the count of five. Ask the actors to feel it out, maybe they are more comfortable with the count of six or four—but find their slow motion breath.

- Once they have found it, ask them to begin to match it to their footfalls. Ask them put their attention on their feet, how one foot launches up and forward, lands on the heel and rolls forward through the midfoot until it reaches the forefoot. Then feel the launch begin in the toes. Note how the launch in the toes coincides with the heel strike of the other foot. Ask them to take their time and focus on really feeling the weight change, the roll through the foot, the launch and to connect the breath to the feet in a pattern, whatever pattern is comfortable to them.

- Ask them to keep their eyes open with a soft focus and that when they get to the end of the room, or a wall or another person, what changes and how can they keep the breath and footfall consistent through the change. Ask them to incorporate sitting or standing when they are ready, or maybe even moving in tandem with one another. If possible, if the whole group can move together in some way at the beginning or end of the exercise, this can be helpful. This can be coached by you directly or merely suggested and then let the actors find it on their own.

- Use a bell or a chime to indicate the end of this exercise. When they hear the bell, ask them to come to a circle in the middle of the stage and sit down, ready for you to talk to them about the rehearsal or for a general check in before rehearsal.

- After the first time you do this exercise, you won't need to coach them through and, in fact, this may be a great way to begin each new rehearsal or class. Let them know ahead of time what is happening, maybe at the end of the first rehearsal in which you use this exercise. This way they will be prepared for the next rehearsal. Tell them at the next rehearsal they should:

- Chat with each other or do what they need (check and turn off cell phones, eat or get water, change, use the bathroom, etc.) outside of the space in a green room or hallway. This creates a 'sacred space' for you to work in, which helps establish an atmosphere of focus and concentration. When rehearsal is about to begin, coach them to silently enter the space, put down their bags, take off their shoes and begin the walking meditation until they hear the bell, at which point they should come to sit down in a circle.
- I suggest 5–10 minutes, but you can also do as little as 3 minutes of walking to prepare your actors to work. When the meditation ends, they will be in a focused place to begin your rehearsal or class.

Actors engaged in Walking Meditation 1.
Credit: Gordon Wenzel

(continued)

(*continued*)

Another way to utilize walking meditation is through the use of fast movement, exploding out of a common stillness. This is often a wonderful way to begin warm ups.

Coach the Walking Meditation 2:

- Before beginning, explain what is going to happen. Then after the explanation is done, begin the exercise and just watch without coaching. Explain:

  - Everyone will join a standing circle in the middle of the stage when, and only when, they are ready to work. Each person will come up in their own time.
  - When the last person joins the group, ask them to feel the desire to move swelling in the group until it becomes unbearable and then as soon as they feel a collective shift (it happens like a bang!), they should all move into full speed walking at the same time.
  - Tell them to move at full speed, but walk. Walking keeps the energy high without the risk of uncontrolled movement/injury.
  - Once they have moved at a fast pace for a bit they will begin to slow down. They will decide when this happens on their own and also as a group—tell them to 'feel' it out, paying attention to their own instincts but also allowing for input from the group.
  - Instruct actors to find the place where the slow-down begins, very subtle at first, then growing until their fast walk becomes a normal pace, and then their normal pace becomes slow motion. Let each actor find this on their own, but most likely the movement of the group will influence everyone as well as the very atmosphere or 'feeling' of the space as a whole.
  - Once they are in slow motion, ask them to again move as before in the walking meditation 1—with breath attached to movement.

- When the 'slow-down' begins to approach stillness, tell them to once again find their place in the circle (could be the same place, could be a different place than before) only this time sitting. Again, they will feel this 'slow-down' on their own and also as a group. The facilitator can sit in the circle at any time, either from the beginning or at the end after everyone else is seated.

- I also find that if you would like to have some gentle control over when the slow-down begins to come to a place of stillness, that the facilitator intentionally sitting down in the circle at a certain time gently suggests that it is time to do so to the whole group who may wish to linger longer than you have time for and they don't realize it is time to move on. This can happen for individuals or even for the group as a whole. Facilitators should also 'feel it out' as they may be the only ones looking at a watch.

Actors engaged in Walking Meditation 2, before the group shifts from stillness to motion.

Credit: Gordon Wenzel

Exercise 5.3 The Matrix

Based on MC's Tool Concentration

Then entire first chapter of Chekhov's *Lessons for Teachers of his Acting Technique* (transcribed by his student Deirdre Hurst du Prey) is dedicated to concentration. Chekhov states:

> Everyone has the power of concentration to some extent but that is not enough for our work. You may have a group of geniuses, but if they have no concentration their talent will be lost. While on the other hand, people with less talent but real concentration will hold your interest. The East knows the secret but the West does not and must learn.[3]

Chekhov directly connects the power of performer concentration to their ability to hold the audience's attention.

When working on a NTS&P production, concentration becomes paramount to the success of finding the arc of the play, as well as finding the physicalization of each individual actor's character arc. As a society, our general focus and concentration skills are low. We are a country of multitasking which of course actually means 'switch-tasking' or switching back and forth since humans are incapable of holding any two ideas in their head at the exact same moment. Clear, focused, extended concentration is a skill that needs to be built. For actors this skill can mean the difference between holding an audience's attention and letting it drift. In a non-traditionally staged production, this is even more prominent because oftentimes the 'blocking' of the piece does not support the story without strong focus from the actors. When actors are fully engaged, and can remain so throughout the piece, then blocking actually becomes more fluid and the dynamic between the actors shines through. This is why in some NTS-style theatre, blocking is relative but need for the dynamic is constant. You could shift the entire ground plan and blocking of a scene in any direction for any audience when the dynamic between the actors is sound. The scene would remain just as strong. Building actor's ability to concentrate then becomes essential to the success of the performance.

In the movie *The Matrix*, Keanu Reeves's character begins to think things into reality once he learns that he is special, that what he imagines can alter the world around him. The key component of his work is concentration. It is also one of the key components of our work. Concentration is essential to the process of engaged and inspired performance, the kind of performance the NTS dynamic requires.

Coaching The Matrix

Based on Chekhov's Concentration Exercises

Objective: To activate and train actor concentration.

If you have just completed the seated meditation exercise and if you won't be doing the second walking meditation, consider an energizing warm-up as a transition if you are launching next into concentration. One way to do this is with a simple game of tag. Blob Tag, Amoeba Tag, Band Aid Tag, Elbow Tag—there are many resources on the web that can help you find new and exciting tag games to get the ensemble moving. The idea is that getting the energy stimulated after relaxing will engage the concentration more successfully because it requires an act of will, not release (what the meditation will have just done for your cast). Jumpstart your cast with a warm-up, if not tag, then have them circle the building once or twice, play travelling follow the leader, whatever it takes to re-engage the mind and body in a playful yet vibrant state of readiness.

Coach Matrix Pt. 1—Imagination:

- Once the ensemble is feeling very present and in the moment from an energizer, have your actors sit down (or stand) in a comfortable place where they can hear you (circles are good) and then instruct them to close their eyes.
- Have them imagine the following (for younger actors, have them imagine, like in *The Matrix*, that they are training their mind to change their reality).

  - As you are instructed to do so, imagine each image as it comes to you.

(continued)

(continued)

- If I give you the word 'dog,' allow the first image that comes to your head be the one to work with. Do not spend time looking for the right or perfect dog. Trust your imagination.
- See the image in your mind's eye (fill in).
- A horse next to a tree. Now merge them together.
- A clock and water. Now merge them together.
- A princess and a spider, now merge the two into one creature.
- A horse running backwards.
- Someone drinking a glass of water. Now backwards.
- A seed. Now imagine it growing from a small sprout into a mighty tree.

- Many of these are directly taken from Michael Chekhov's work, but feel free to create your own as well. Any images will do!

Coach Matrix Pt. 2—Merging:

- Now coach your actors to open their eyes and look around the room. Find a place in the room that feels good. Ask your actors to look at that place and send their attention toward that place.
- Coach them that this is a two-way street and as they are sending their energy toward the spot, the spot is sending the energy back to them. Ask them to begin to 'merge' with the spot with their imaginations (images, feelings, textures and colors may come up for some—tell them to incorporate these ideas in any way they like!).
- Ask them to keep merging until they have successfully merged with the spot. Advise them that there is no right or wrong way to do this; they are just looking to feel that they are 'with' the spot or that they have the 'essence' of the spot clearly in their imaginations.
- Once they have successfully merged, have them walk around the room still holding the spot with them, as the new merged actor/spot entity. They do not have to be looking at the spot after that. Ask them to note how the merging might affect how they move, see the other actors, speak to each other.

- Ask the actors to pay special attention to the way the spot affects their whole body from the back and sides as well as the front, always keeping the whole body resonating instead of just the face, just the torso or just the front of their body. If they begin to lose the spot, tell them they can at any time return to the spot to absorb it more fully and/or look at the spot to absorb from where they are.
- Then let them let that spot go.
- Ask them to then perform the exercise again with a new spot. This time with a 'lonely' spot. Have them get closer to the spot this time as they send their focus. Then once again have them walk around the room and either speak or make contact or at least see the other people in the room.
- Have them find one more spot in the room and follow the same instructions—this spot could be a weird spot or a classy spot or anything. Just one that is 'calling' to them (or their imaginations) to explore.
- Once they have gone through all three spots, ask them to phys-ically go back to the one that they found most interesting to embody. Have them merge with the spot one more time and then have them play a tag game. If you have played one before in class or in rehearsal, go back to that one. It should not be too hard to master, just a physical exercise they can try from the point of view of the new character they have created by merg-ing with a spot in the room.
- Have them play this game while still holding the spot, as the new merged actor/spot entity. Have them play the game again (or a different tag type game) and try one of the other two merged spot characters they found from earlier. If they have lost the idea, tell them they can at any point return to the actual spot to retrieve the merged image and then return to the game after.
- After the game is over, have your actors circle together and discuss what surprised them. Ask what they found exciting or interesting or even just fun. These exercises in deep concentra-tion often benefit from a discussion period after speaking about what it means to 'hold' an idea or image in your head and body

(continued)

(*continued*)

for an extended amount of time. Ask them how this related to both building and maintaining characters both intellectually and physically.

Coach Matrix Pt. 3—Advanced:

Here is an advanced variation of the exercise from Lisa Loving Dalton.

- Starting once again with a singular spot: "Imagine/pretend there is an elastic band (string, ribbon, thread) attached to your IAC, connecting it to the spot. Begin to move slowly, in any direction, sensing kinesthetically and visualizing how the tension varies as you move closer or further from the spot. Gradually increase the tempo, vary the levels, change the rhythms of the movements."
- "What happens to the ribbon when you turn away from your spot? Imagine that your body is sheer and so the ribbon need not wrap around you. It is always able to have a direct line from your center, through any body part, to the spot."
- To begin, the artists play freely in their own world, amongst the class, so that initially, the other artists don't affect each other. After playing solo, add into the mix an awareness of the contact that other actors have on your elastic ribbon. When one actor moves between you and your spot, what happens to your ribbon and you? What are the possible things that could happen?
- When ready, go back to playing solo, and add another spot in a polar direction and play as above. Gradually add spot #3, and then #4, again in polar directions. One can add as many as one likes. If the playing space has balconies or an orchestra pit, be sure to include those levels, too.
- A further advance of this concentration and spatial awareness exercise is the possibility of coloring the elastic bands/spots with qualities. For example, imagine a color wheel in Photoshop where the center of the wheel is neutral. Slide in any direction, responding to the color changes. Use emotional qualities, textures, etc.

Give your actors homework to merge objects in their imagination or merge *with* objects in their physical imagination and then allow themselves to experiment with any number of new merged actor/ spot entities. Remind them that they don't actually have to 'feel' anything (remember that song from the show *A Chorus Line*?) but rather encourage them to enjoy the place of 'what if' or 'make believe' as they did as children. It is also okay if some actors do actually feel some of what they create. Some actors have incredible mind–body connections and those should also be nurtured and encouraged as creative resources, so long as the actor is reminded to always be safe. Have actors consider the rich physical choices that bubble to the surface when they allow themselves to imagine with 'what if' or allow themselves to connect deeply to their imaginations. If they are so inclined, it is a wonderful continuation of this exercise to draw these images and/or ideas as pictures or collages in a journal or notebook. Or perhaps have actors write a poem about the merging or the merged item. Maybe write a monologue or a dialogue between the items as they merge or between two merged items (or people) or one merged and one unmerged item. The possibilities are limitless. Actors can keep these creations for themselves or bring these explorations to share with you or the whole ensemble.

A Note on Safety

For me, being safe with the images and ideas we explore as actors means always being mindful of what we dwell on for extended amounts of time and taking into consideration if anything feels harmful or painful in anyway. Those areas should be avoided and/ or explored carefully with a very real sense of caution on the part of the actor as well as the facilitator. The old adage, 'If anything hurts stop doing it' would be a key guideline here.

If you cannot afford to avoid such images or ideas (if for instance those images are a vital part of the play you are exploring), ask actors to only explore those images in rehearsal with you and end the exercises exploring these topics with 'palate' cleansing rituals, such as an energizing game (like tag) or another Chekhov exploration/exercise or (one of my favorites) a 'Not Dance Party.'

Be sure to have your music ready and coach actors to not dance, but rather to move to the music—inspired by Wil Kilroy's Exercise 4.4 'Filling Space: The Full Body Dance.' Call out body parts for them to explore with—for example, "Explore the music with your feet! Your hands! How do your hands affect the rest of your body? Your knees!"—until by the end they explore with their whole body. 'Not Dancing' allows the actors to not have to worry about a correct form or popular way of dancing and rather just allow their bodies to let loose in the moment and joyfully (we hope) physically explore and play in the space. This I have found is an excellent way to disperse any difficult imagery or ideas that stick in the mind and body after an intense exercise is over. Be sure to pick fun, playful music of any genre.

Exercise 5.4 Ball Work

Based on MC's Tool The Four Brothers

You may have encountered some kind of ball work at some point during your own theatre training. The use of the ball as a training tool is historic; Michael Chekhov employed it during his work at the Actor Training Program at Dartington Hall and even earlier with the Moscow Art Theatre. Ball work was used then, and is so often used now because as a tool it is flexible and multifunctional, providing many different benefits to a class or an ensemble. It can be used for many different kinds of Chekhov training in particular.

Actors engaged in Ball Work.
Credit: Gordon Wenzel

It can help in learning names to create a feeling ensemble (if done on the very first day), engage a state of readiness (when you add many balls), train the attention (when you work in a pattern, or many different patterns with different balls, or then go backwards in the patterns) or even engender a feeling of trust (when at some point in the pattern you ask them to let go of the circle and just move about the room—don't worry, your partners are all still here!). Below we use the ball work to help train and further define the Four Brothers of Peak Performance.

'The Four Brothers' are described by Michael Chekhov as qualities present in actors in moments of peak performance.

The four brothers are:

1. A Feeling of Ease (an actor's lightness to all movement, even character heaviness).
2. A Feeling of Form (the shape of the body, attention to body/bodies in space, body in relation to the environment, to other bodies, etc.).
3. A Feeling of Beauty (that which is striking/arresting to the imagination).
4. A Feeling of the Whole (a beginning, middle and end to everything onstage).

These four qualities work together to create deeply resonant moments, dynamic relationships and strong authenticity onstage. These concepts are foundational in the performance, particularly so in NTS&P productions.

Coaching Ball Work

Based on Chekhov's Four Brothers and his Dartington Hall Ball Exercises

Objective: To prepare actors for peak performance.

Coaching Ball Work Pt. 1:

- Bring in a bag of four or five different kinds of balls—yarn balls, bouncy balls, hacky sack balls, balls that flash, different color

(continued)

(*continued*)

balls, whiffle balls, etc. They should all be about hand size or larger and none of them should be too heavy or hard.

- Use one ball to start each exercise, and when multiple balls are called for use, no more than five balls for 8–16 people and four balls for 4–8 people. If you have a large cast of more than 16, you may consider breaking the group into two circles at first and then adding them together at the end.

A Feeling of the Whole: The Full Exchange

- When actors are standing in a circle, have them begin tossing just one ball around the circle.
- Ask the actors to pause momentarily to allow you to jump into the circle to show them how to send and receive the ball while continuing the flow of energy. Demonstrate how to send and receive the ball with no stops, no catches but rather a feeling of drawing the ball into your hand, letting the energy that was sent to you keep your arm moving (as well as the rest of your body in response).
- Allow the energy you are given to transform into something new, make eye contact with a person across the circle and send it on. Once you have demonstrated this technique, step out of the circle and have the actors continue sending and receiving the ball.
- As they get accustomed to this exchange of energy, ask them to think about how the ball comes to them, and to start looking more closely at the receiving and transforming part of the interaction. Each moment has a beginning (the receive), a middle (the transformation) and the end (the search for a new receiver and sending it on).
- Have them observe without judgment when they miss steps. Did someone forget to find someone's eyes before sending it on? Did someone not receive the energy that was sent to them by stopping the ball? Did someone skip the transformation and skip right to the send? Encourage them to 'find the flow of energy' and especially to give each moment a clear beginning, middle and end. Ask them also to observe without

judgment if they are habitually sending and receiving in the same way. What happens when you change it up? Invite them to be adventurous.

- Connect this idea to the idea of giving and receiving onstage. In every moment onstage actors are either receiving, transforming, sending or in a state of readiness to receive. Ask what happens when steps are missed in the ball game and onstage. How does 'A Feeling of the Whole' contribute to a peak performance experience for the audience?

A Feeling of Beauty: Everything is a Choice,
There Are No 'Non-Choices'

- As the actors continue to pass the first ball with a feeling of the whole, ask them to keep doing that but now to add their names. They should say their name as they pass the ball, saying it and sending it to the person across the circle that they select.

An Actor engaged in Ball Work.
Credit: Gordon Wenzel

(continued)

(continued)

- Encourage them to allow for an expansion of the name; they should begin saying their name once they make eye contact with the person they are throwing it to. Then they should wind up and keep saying their name until it is caught.
- Once they are comfortable with that, begin to encourage them to play with the way their name sounds. Send something particular to the person through your voice. And as you receive something from someone, let it affect you and give you something (through the transformation) that will affect the way you send it to the next person.
- Slowly add another ball in while they are playing. And then another and another until you have four or five balls in play. At first they will be nervous adding new balls, but eventually they will relax and have fun being very much in the moment, open to whatever is coming their way. With many balls it also becomes hard for them to 'pre plan' what their response will be or to worry about how they are doing.
- They will need all their attention on keeping an eye on all the balls sailing through the air. When balls fall, as they always do, encourage the actors that the goal of the game is not to catch each ball perfectly but to make something out of whatever comes to you. So how will they choose to recover from a fallen ball, how will it transform and affect how they send it on. Ask them now to find the form of each moment as it comes, trying not to rush the feeling of the whole but also allowing themselves to be open to whatever comes to them. The goal is to find a place of creating in the moment an authentic kinesthetic response. But one with a clear choice of form. A beginning, middle and end but with an eye to the shape the moment takes.
- Encourage them to find the beauty in the names. That which is striking, arresting. The power that it holds. Ask them to attach images to the name as they send it. What arises? What do you send? Lastly, ask them to invest in a feeling of gratitude for this name they were given, this life, this body, this journey—which all began with their name. Ask them to find their place in the

Actors engaged in Ball Work.

Credit: Gordon Wenzel

world by sharing their name, sharing who they are deep within, through the ball toss.

- Variations. Have them pass the name of the person they are sending the energy to. Have them pass their own character names. Have them say the name of the character they are sending their energy to. And then ask the same big questions in terms of beauty.

A Feeling of Form: It's Not What You Said, It's How You Said It!

- In the same session, have everyone switch places and find a new spot in the circle. Start at the beginning with one ball. Remind them to work toward a feeling of the whole (beginning, middle and end/receive, transform, send on) and a feeling of beauty (a definite choice in delivery, bestowed with intent). You can have them use their names, each other's names or names from the play to start, but make sure voices are engaged. By the end, have them using each other's names or character names of the person they are sending the ball to.
- Once the first ball has gone around to everyone at least three or four times, ask the person holding the ball to stop as you explain the next part. Tell them that this first ball is a 'high' ball and those throwing the ball must make their voice and/or their body high in some way. They must still work toward making sure the other person can catch the ball but attention to 'high' must be paid.

(continued)

(continued)

- Then begin the game again. Once they have gotten used to the high ball, show the next ball, which should be very different in color, texture or kind from your first ball. Do not use balls that can be easily confused for each other. Tell them this second ball is the 'low' ball. Same rules apply. The high ball is still in play. Go! Next periodically stop the game and add more balls, giving them titles and/or actions. Here are some choices of potential balls:

  - *Bad Dialect Ball.* The person who gets this ball must respond in dialect and they must give the impression they are from that region physically. We call it the bad dialect because the goal is not to be perfect with the dialect or even the physical interpretation but to play with being someone else. The dialects don't have to make sense or even be from a real place, they just have to commit and have fun with them.
  - *Whiny Ball.* The person who gets this ball must be send it on with a whine and they must also let their body whine physically as well.
  - *Cheerleader Ball.* The person who gets this ball has to leave their place in the circle, run all the way around the whole circle once all the while cheering the person's name the ball is intended for. Once they have made it around the circle once, they continue around again until they find the person, hand it off and take their place.
  - *Under the Wire Ball.* The person who gets this ball must get across the middle of the circle to a person on the other side to deliver their ball. They can crawl, roll, hop or move in any way they like so long as they stay low to the ground. They can match their sound/name to the way they are moving. If they are hit with a ball during this changeover, they must 'die a horrible death' and then ghost their way to the next person.
  - *Cartoon Ball.* The person who gets this ball must use a cartoon voice and/or countenance to send the ball on.

- *Musical Ball.* The person who gets this ball must sing it to the next person. They should sing as if in a musical with their whole self.
- *Super Secret Spy Ball.* The person who gets this ball must hold on to it secretly for a few tosses and then try somehow to pass it to the next person without anyone noticing. The pass does not have to be across the circle.
- *Angry Parent Ball.* The person who gets this ball must deliver it to the next person like an angry parent.
- *Crushing Pre-Teen Ball.* The person who gets this ball must deliver it as if they have a huge crush on the person they are sending it to.
- *Master of Time and Space Ball/Phoenix Ball.* The person who gets this ball steps out of the circle, either through or around, and in slow motion delivers the ball to the next person and takes their place in the circle. If they are hit with a ball during this changeover, they must 'die a horrible death' and then be reborn anew to pass the ball on.

- As the ensemble works continue to remind them to pay attention to the feeling of the whole (beginning, middle and end), the feeling of beauty (definite full choices with each moment) and now give careful attention to feeling of form (the way they choose to transform by what is given to them).

Actors engaged in Ball Work.
Credit: Gordon Wenzel

(*continued*)

(continued)

Feeling of Ease: I Got This

- Begin again with just one ball from the top. Ask them to say the name of the person they are throwing to as they throw, or their character (decide on one and have everyone follow suit). Then, before beginning, have everyone hold up their hand.
- Have the ball go around the circle once, each person throwing to another person who has their hand up. If a person has their hand down, the ball has already come to them. Have the actors pay special attention to who they get the ball from and who they are sending it on to.
- Once the ball has gone around once, ask the actors to repeat the sequence. If they get lost, ask them to put the ball down and point at the person they received the ball from. Now point at the person they will send the ball to—if they are confused, ask them to help each other. There is no 'cheating' on this. Then have them do the whole sequence through pointing. Next have them go back to the ball.
- Once they are comfortable with this sequence, have them put the first ball down. And use a new ball to set a new sequence following the exact same directions.
- When they are comfortable with the new sequence, add the first ball in again so that now they are working two balls through two distinct sequences. If and when they get tense, encourage them to let go of unnecessary tension in the body and to just know that it will all work out. Ask them to find the feeling of ease as they move through the sequences, when everything just clicks and it's almost as if they are going on instinct.
- Remind them to give their motions a beginning, middle and end (Feeling of the Whole), to make choices on how to send energy on (Feeling of Beauty), to pay attention to the sequence (Feeling of Form) and finally to give every movement a Feeling of Ease, so even if you are tense on the inside, then from the outside this is easy, light and playful. Let them know they can 'fake' this feeling but they must show us that this is no big deal.

- Once they feel comfortable, add a third and fourth ball/ sequence to the game. There will be times when one person gets more than one ball, maybe even all four. Remind them that the goal is not to be perfect but play and that they will have more chances to handle the situation when it arises again.
- Once they have gotten somewhat comfortable with all four balls, ask them now to leave the circle but keep passing. When they panic, encourage them that no one is leaving the game, that the person will be there for them to pass it on. Have them walk around the room. They can decide to toss or hand over the ball any way they see fit. Encourage them to keep embracing the four brothers as they move.
- Find a place to end.

Once they end this final component of the four-part exercise, ask when they were most comfortable and when they weren't. What does it mean to show a feeling of ease? Go back over the four brothers with the ensemble and ask for moments in which little surprises bubbled to the top. What were they? At the end open up the discussion, how is passing the ball like doing a play? How do the four brothers' ball play moments relate to moments onstage. Hopefully some 'Ahas!' will appear through the discussion.

Exercises 5.5 Origin and 5.6 Suitcase

Based on MC's Tool Centers

Many professional performers and students of acting may be familiar with the concept of centers. Locating a region or 'spot' in your body from which all movement originates. A person 'leads' with their center. Choosing different centers to explore when working on a new character allows actors to experiment with physicality. The Chekhov Technique takes the exercise further by allowing actors not only to explore the 'spot' from which all movement originates (any place in the body is fair game for this) but also the quality of the spot itself. The power of attaching qualities and images to centers, and their requisite effect on the body, cannot be oversold.

In an arena staging, this deep commitment to physicality that comes as a result of 'playing' with images through the body allows for some gorgeously rendered characters that can resonate from every angle. A man who leads with his forehead is one thing to see on stage, but a man who leads from the bullet between his eyes often allows for a far more specific physicality from the actor, one that can be shared through the back and sides of the body as well as the front. The first feels almost literal. The second, far more metaphoric, allowing for all parts of the body to participate in the interpretation. There is also the option of the moving center. The moving center allows actors to work between two distinct centers, allowing for a more nuanced contradiction housed within the body. Any of these centers can also be further developed with attention to veiling—the degree to which you reveal the inner movement of your character (while remaining consistent in the degree of energy with which you express this movement). This complex rendering of the character can be a powerful tool when engaging NTS work.

Coaching Origin

Based on Chekhov's Qualities of Movement and Centers

Objective: To explore detailed and nuanced character physicality.

Coach:

- Begin by asking the ensemble to move through the space releasing unnecessary tension in their body by allowing their shoulders to roll up and back and then release.
- Have them pull up through the spine, but not too stiff, with a slight bend at the knee and their head facing forward, eyes off the ground—soft focus.
- Have them imagine their 'centers' as the place where they are being pulled forward from, the origin point of their movement across the space. Ask them to place this center in their chest.
- In placing their energetic attention in this location in their body, reveal to them they are engaging their Ideal Artistic Center.

Note on the Ideal Artistic Center

NMCA describes the Ideal Artistic Center (IAC) as a warm center of energy just at the level of your heart but in the center of your chest. This is in contrast to the idea of 'neutral,' which is touted as the standard place to begin in many acting programs, but which can be perceived differently by different people. The IAC is lifted, balanced and crisp. The gait is easy and energized. This center encourages the performer to be present and encourages the audience to watch. This specific physicality is in contrast to the idea of a 'blank slate,' which can be as confusing as 'color-blind' casting. There is no actor that can achieve a true blank slate status, just as there is no audience that has a neutral response to ethnicity and race. The idea behind both ideas is a kind of altruistic common neutrality for all, but in reality, it is unattainable. The IAC provides a strong alternative, inviting the actor to come to an energetic and open place to begin.

- Allow them to drop back into their regular gait and examine what the difference is.
- Is their 'center point' different? Does their energy seem to pull from a different area?
- Move them through this exercise a few times snapping back into their 'IAC' and then back to their regular walk.
- Once they find the IAC, this should begin to become easy for them, ask them to snap in and out of the IAC at will.
- Once they are comfortable with this, as they are walking in their natural way, have them watch each other while they walk.
- Once they have done that for some time, ask them to pick one person in the room without letting them know and identify their center, their origin of movement.
- Once they have spent time observing it, ask them to transform their own natural center into the center they see in their fellow ensemble member.
- They do not have to walk or move like the person they selected (although that may happen) but to just instead experiment with what it feels like to be lead from a new place.

(continued)

(continued)

- Right from here, allow actors to return to their IAC and then ask them imagine one of their parents or a family member.
- Have them imagine that person walking, moving, sitting up or laying down. Have the actors assess where their family member's center is and ask them to take on that center.
- Have them try a few more on for size—another family member, a best friend, someone they dislike or are annoyed by, someone they trust, someone they do not trust, someone they admire, someone they fear, someone they pity, etc.

Note: At this point it is often a good point to stop and reflect—what discoveries were made? Any insights into the people whose centers you were working with? In what way does the movement from the center define the person more clearly for you?

- Once initial reflections are made, ask them to move around the room again, and this time call out centers to them—lead from the knee, right ear, cheek, eyes, mouth, left chin, elbows, forehead, butt (still moving forward) back of the knees, etc.
- Move through these slower at first and ask them what kind of person might move this way. Who could live in this body?
- Once they are used to the exercise, pick up speed, forcing them to assess the uninhibited response rather than try to find the 'right' intellectual answer.
- Find a place to end and reflect again. What discoveries were made? What kind of people rose to the surface?

Coaching Suitcase

Based on Chekhov's Ideas on Centers

Objective: To build strong and deeply motivated character physicality.

Coach the List:

- Have your ensemble pull out a piece of paper and a pencil or pen. This part can also be done as homework and then brought into rehearsal that day.

- Then instruct them to write a list of items for their character, but not just an inventory or moving list. Have them create the suitcase list: the most important possessions must go in the suitcase.
- These are the sentimental ones, the ones that mean something significant, the ones that can't be replaced. These are the items you pack when witness protection tells you that you can never come back to the house. Or the items you pack when, as Lisa Dalton once had to do, wildfires are raging near your home and you must pack what only what you can carry and only what is most meaningful.
- Have them imagine what those things could be for their character. These items could come directly from the text play but they don't have to. They can be imagined items as an extension of what you know about the character and the play. They don't have to 'make sense.' If you feel a very powerful character wants to carry a teddy bear, allow that to go on the list. No one has to see this private list, and you don't have to work out why they have it right now. If it pops up in your head as something they may want for some reason, write it down.
- Once you have written these physical objects down, add to the list with 'lost items.' Items the character no longer has but wishes they could put in the suitcase. Same rules apply, don't question—just write down. Once you have those, write about five photographs your character packs in the suitcase. What are they of? Who or where? Why doesn't matter right now. Just write the list. Once the cast has the list down, have them set the paper down and set it off to the side in the working space for a bit.

Coach Centers with Qualities:

- Now coach the ensemble to once again move around the space as they did in the 'Origin' exercise. First moving in their natural way, then finding their artistic center, then moving back and forth between the two, noting the differences.
- Then begin to give them centers to play with, nose, hips, stomach, shoulder blades, back of the neck, left hand, toes, etc.

(*continued*)

(continued)

- Once they are moving quickly through those, slow down and begin to attach qualities to each body part you name. It often helps if the facilitator writes these down ahead of time. Here are some examples:

  - Warm nose
  - Sweaty small of the back
  - Sticky fingers
  - Cold chest
  - Smooth cheekbones.

- Now begin to attach images to each center. Here again, a list in your hand beforehand is helpful (even better if you already have ideas for some of the characters threaded in).

- Coach, 'Let yourself be led from' or 'Imagine the center as,' for example:

  - A small pink ball of yarn unrolling from your eyes
  - An uncomfortable tree branch in your spine
  - Soft sand in your calves
  - Warm moist black earth between your toes
  - Fat cold snowflakes behind your ears.

- Make sure to give them some examples that are very close together to note differences, such as:

  - Red velvet in your hips
  - Black velvet in your hips
  - Yellow silk in your hips.

- Don't back away from the uncomfortable, for example:

  - A dead fish in your jaw
  - A bloody rag on your back
  - An unused baby shoe in the small of your hand.

- Or the silly:

  - Bubbles in your butt
  - Glitter in your hair
  - Soggy cereal in your knees.

- Allow yourself to move beyond body parts to places of the body:

    - Hot coffee in your smile
    - Tinkling ice cubes in your gaze
    - A sunny window in your heart.

- Once you begin to move into the metaphoric, begin to move into imagery that is not static. Start with the static image and then give it life.

Coach other Moving Images:

- Imagine your center as a butterfly pinned to your throat. Now imagine that the butterfly is still alive, but pinned there, moving its wings softly, softly.
- Other examples may include:

    - Moths trapped in your stomach
    - A ball bouncing between your stomach and your heart (maybe a red ball? a yellow ball?)
    - Sand leaking out of your smile into your chest.

Coach Advanced Image Centers Pt. 1:

- Coach actors to imagine their center in their heart. As they get comfortable with that, tell them to imagine their heart no longer in their body but just in front of them. Open. Vulnerable. Now have them move with that center outside of their body. Begin to increase the distance, moving the heart farther away.
- When they are ready, tell them to place their heart across the room in someone else's body. Keep moving around feeling that heart outside of you. Then have them imagine that person leaving the room with their center still inside them. Imagine them leaving with their heart.
- Now tell your actors to clear the image and allow themselves to take the time to restore their hearts back to themselves before they relax and let go of the exercise.
- Once you have moved through this sequence, reflect as a group talking about discoveries made and what surprises they

(*continued*)

(continued)

may have found. It is often helpful to ask one observation from each person. It is also helpful for you as the facilitator of the exercise to tell the ensemble what you observed, things that surprised you or held your attention deeply. Once the discussion is over, have them go back to their suitcase list and pick three items from their list to experiment with. To end this session, have them get on their feet and try these three items in different parts of the body.

Coach Suitcase Pt. 2:

• Have actors begin with one item from their suitcase. Place this item in the IAC. Allow the item to stay here or to move to another place in the body, a place that feels like 'home' for this object, for this character.
• Allow the actors to let the image of the object affect them. Ask them to invest deeply in its qualities—is it warm or cold, heavy or light, soft or hard—how does this affect their movement around the room?
• Now have them put that item in a difference place opposite to the one they just picked. Again work with its qualities; maybe try new ones—different ones. Now have actors place it in a third random place in the body and work with that.
• Have actors repeat this sequence for all three items. At first let go of each item fully before you add the next. As this exercise develops, you may find using multiple layered images in one center provides interesting results and/or placing images in different parts of the body at the same time may also provide interesting results. Allow the actors to have choices if you return to this exercise more than once. The first time, however, keep it simple—let go of one before working on the next.
• Now ask the actors to pick the item and the center placement that most resonated with them. Begin to work with veiling and ask them to allow us to see how the object affects the movement at a 5, 8, 10, 2, 5, 4, 1, etc.

- Bring them to a one: revealed from only the IAC but still active through the back, the sides and behind the eyes. Then ask them to do simple tasks with that center—sitting down, laying down, standing up, greeting or talking to each other briefly, etc.

Lastly, allow for one more discussion and reflection. What discoveries were made about characters and movement? Ask the actors to continue their explorations (images, qualities of images, their centers and movement of those centers) as they continue to develop their characters. It is often helpful to give a deadline for when you might meet with them individually to discuss what they are interested in for these centers. Perhaps you could ask them to show you three discoveries and then you can work together as director and actor to pick which centers really resonate with the concept and interpretation you have for the play. You may even decide to use all of them at different points in the play. This exercise alone can lead to some of the most beautiful and poetic interpretations for the character you have yet seen, born of an image and then carried out exquisitely, physically and from all sides.

Exercise 5.7 From Stillness to Chaos: Physical Rhythms

Based on MC's Tool Tempo

Tempo, the speed at which a performance should be played, is a tool Chekhov employs as a creative character-building device. He utilizes this tool in tandem with the idea of qualities:

> Different tempos change the qualities and even the meaning of an action. A simple example can explain this. Say 'Goodbye' or 'How do you do' in different tempos you will see how the qualities of these words and even the meaning of the departure or the meeting will change with the tempo. Any action, however complicated it may be, will change with the tempo. That means an actor can use tempo not only as a means of shaping a (performance) but also as a means of awakening and enriching his feelings and his inner life on the stage.[4]

In the following exercise, Wil Kilroy introduces the idea of tempo as means to the creative exploration of physicality.

Coaching From Stillness to Chaos

Based on Chekhov's Ideas on Tempo

By Wil Kilroy

Objective: By exploring a variety of rhythms, the actor will be ready to embody a diverse group of characters that express themselves in multiple ways.

Coach:

- Actors begin by finding a comfortable spot in the space standing, and are then instructed to simply experience stillness.
- Be aware of what stillness feels like in the body. Do you have the desire to fidget? Is it difficult to be still? This is a skill that can be developed. Stillness is not the absence of energy but only the absence of movement. Perhaps the senses are even more heightened as you remain still.
- What do you hear? What's happening with your breath? What do you sense against your skin? Against the soles of your feet?
- From here, the actors are instructed to begin moving in a legato manner—smooth and flowing. Actors need to have that legato quality in their feet, in every step, and move with large abstract gestures in order to experience the legato energy in every part of the body.
- Next guide the actors to change their movements to staccato— short, sudden and sharp. Again, be sure to encourage the staccato energy to be in every part of their body—the shifting of their eyes in a new direction and the way they lift their foot to step.
- Next the actors move in a lyrical fashion—a combination of legato, staccato and perhaps even moments of stillness but in a graceful pattern such as a waltz.
- Then suddenly, instruct the actors to burst into chaos. There is no pattern, no determined tempo, but unbridled energy expressing itself in all directions.

- Then bring the actors back to stillness and then tell them to relax.
- Next, pair actors with partners (can be a threesome if necessary) and tell them they can improvise dialogue in each of the five rhythms—allowing stillness just enough energy to be able to speak, and chaos to have just enough focus to be able to converse.
- Use a bell or some other system to indicate choosing another partner in the group—improvise a new dialogue with a new rhythm. Keep changing partners until everyone has tried the five rhythms at least once. Sometimes actors will pair with actors of the same energy, sometimes of different energies—both are suitable.
- If you have time, after the initial five, allow actors to switch rhythms within the same conversation. Where is the transition point? Why?
- After the actors have rotated through at least five rhythms, have them reflect on what they discovered in the improvisation. Then ask them to consider the energies of their character.

Exercise 5.8 Experience the Rhythm: Real and Imagined Music

Based on MC's Tool Tempo

Returning to our explorations utilizing Chekhov's tools on Tempo, in this exercise Wil Kilroy has actors attach specific music to internal and external stimuli, thereby influencing the physicality through the character's reactions to their own personal 'soundtrack.'

Coaching Experience the Rhythm

Based on Chekhov's Idea of Tempo

By Wil Kilroy

Objective: By physically responding to both present and imagined music, actors find a variety of modes of expression, continuing to expand their potential for diverse character creation.

(continued)

(continued)

Coach:

- Actors are asked to move randomly in the space, and a piece of music is played.
- Actors then let themselves be inspired to move in a certain way as a result of the musical cue.
- The music played might be country and western and an old-fashioned hoedown atmosphere might be created via the movements.
- Actors let that go as the piece of music ends and return to walking randomly in the space.
- Another selection is then played which embodies a completely different feel, such as heavy metal. The result might be heads bobbing back and forth in chaos or stomping.
- Once several selections are played, then the actors can be asked to now hear a specific genre of music in their heads (with no music playing) and move with however that inspires them.
- As the leader you might call out "dramatic opera" or "Broadway musical comedy" or "gospel." As always, there is no right or wrong to any actor's response, allowing them to be expressing creatively in response to the imagined music.
- Although this is primarily a physical exercise, if an actor would like to vocalize, encourage them to try this exercise twice, first without sound, then slowly adding breath and voice, thereby focusing on one aspect of the tool clearly before adding another. They can try this in rehearsal and then at home on their own. Be sure to encourage them to bring in any discoveries they make to share with the group (or just you if you prefer).
- When the exercise ends, ask actors to reflect on which genres were difficult and which were easy to hear in their heads. Ask them also to consider if there is a genre that fits their character and how might the movements discovered in the exercise influence the physicality of the character. Ask them to be specific! Encourage them to continue to explore these discoveries in scene rehearsals as well.

Exercise 5.9 Inner/Outer Friction

Based on MC's Idea of Tempo

In connection to the excellent tool from Wil Kilroy, another use of tempo that Chekhov employed was inner and outer tempo: "Our usual conception of tempo onstage does not take into consideration its two different aspects, inner and outer. . . . These types of tempo are so different that they can be observed simultaneously, even in cases where they are completely contradictory."[5] This exercise leans into the interesting friction created when a character's inner tempo does not match their outer tempo.

Coaching Inner/Outer Friction

Based on Chekhov's Idea of Tempo

Objective: To find physicality that allows for inner conflict to become clear.

Coach:

- After working through the exercise above, try asking the actors to move about the room while you call out different tempos (legato, staccato, lyrical, chaos, stillness), encouraging them to find new ways of engaging with each tempo.
- At this time, feel free to also utilize the tool of veiling, asking them to "take it to a 3, 6, 2, 7"—seven being the largest most expansive movements and one being the most internal (but still fully energized movement).
- Once you have gone through all five, begin to work different inner and outer movements:

  - Allow yourself to feel legato on the inside but staccato on the outside.
  - Now staccato on the inside but appear legato on the outside.

(continued)

(*continued*)

- Begin to play with all the combinations.
- As the actors become comfortable with that, allow for the veiling tool to come back in:
  - Staccato on the outside, legato on the inside—but let it start to leak out at a 2, 4, 6—can't even hide it now—7!
  - At seven you are at the full expression and then you may bring something else to the inside.
- Afterwards—in discussion, ask the actors what kind of situations might fit each internal/external pairing. Examples include:
  - An audition (legato on the outside, staccato on the inside)
  - A first date (legato on the outside, staccato on the inside)
  - A boring lecture (staccato on the outside, legato on the inside)
  - Being inebriated but wanting to appear sober (staccato on the outside, legato on the inside)
  - Lying (legato on the outside, staccato on the inside)
  - Your ensemble is sure to come up with many more.

Exercise 5.10 Vroom Vroom, Kid's Play

Inspired by MC's Ideas of Feeling of Ease

Continuing our work on the Four Brothers' tool of 'Feeling of Ease,' Samantha Norton allows us to connect to our vocal cords in nostalgic and imagistic ways that allow for a softening of muscular tension.

Coaching Vroom Vroom, Kid's Play

Inspired by Chekhov's Ideas of Feeling of Ease

By Samantha Norton

Many of my classes include a substantial amount of vocal improvisation. *Vroom Vroom* is one that came from observing children playing with cars, army men, dolls or any other imaginary role-playing game.

Objective: Employing a feeling of ease vocally is the goal of the *Vroom Vroom* exercise.

Coach:

- Have your students get on the floor and imagine playing cars, adding police cars, ambulances, racecars, anything that invites them to engage their voices. Environmental sounds are okay too. Ask your students to keep their voices in the falsetto range light and high. (Having real matchbox cars to play with is also a plus!)
- Have them interact with each other for a few minutes and you'll see how they start to create a vocal world so clear that we 'see' the cars, trucks, etc. even if they aren't there. What is happening pedagogically is that the student is creating sounds to serve the action—not a preconceived notion of what sound should be like. This is an important distinction. Spontaneous sounds that serve the action are free and genuine.
- For a variation, have them play the car game but as aliens or have them replace the cars with a horse ranch where your students create the sounds of hooves, neighing, whistles, dogs barking.
- Remind the students to embody their sounds or others in their bodies, both in action and reaction to others. Warning: this exercise is joyful to watch and do.

If we only have our students standing in a circle and repeating a series of vowel/consonant drills, they are more prone to work with tension (especially the students who want to be heard above everyone else), they also have less of an opportunity to associate sound with action. Remember, our vocal folds and resonators (tongue, jaw, lips) are activated the moment we think of something to say and how to say it so why not give your students every chance to experience sounds and vocalizations without tension.

Advice from the Pros: On Acting and Directing in the Arena—Or, Give Me Back My Third Dimension

By Lynn Musgrave

I understand the primary audience here is actors approaching performing in an arena for the first time; I started as an actor in several arenas; I'm now primarily a director with an occasional turn on the boards, and most of the same rules apply. It's impossible, really, to address actors on arena acting without first addressing how plays are staged in the first place.

After three decades of directing arena theatre, every assignment I take for a proscenium takes me a week just to get my bearings. My three-dimensional world has become two and it's a challenge. I know directors (and actors) new to arena stages are similarly disoriented; what I can tell you, though, is that your very best asset is a set designer experienced in floor plans suited for the arena. Of course, one arena is not another arena; there may be three entrances—four—five—even six. Your challenge is controlling your sightlines—and your focus.

Nine times out of ten, your strongest point of focus is center stage— or as close to "center" as your area design defines. Do not—I repeat— do not rob yourself of that area by plopping some big set piece (a buffet, for example) in the middle of it. The last time a set piece occupied

Lynn Musgrave, director and sound designer.
Credit: Lynn Musgrave

Flaming Guns of the Purple Sage. Directed by Lynn Musgrave. Theatre in the Round, Minneapolis, MN, 2005.

Credit: Theatre in the Round, Minneapolis, MN

that point in one of my productions was Agatha Christie's *Witness for the Prosecution*, given the fact the entire second act features a witness on the stand—but that elevated box doubled as a corner window used frequently in Act I. In other words, you and your set designer need to be very protective of your strongest acting areas.

Now it's time to go back to high school geometry (groan). Your staging, every time you have more than two actors on stage, is going to be based upon triangles. The general rule of thumb for beginning arena directors is to stage actors with their backs toward one entrance/vomitorium (let's call them voms) speaking to another actor with his back toward another one. And the third actor with his back to another—you've created a triangle. You'll soon learn you can manipulate these angles with seated actors (the standing actor should not be blocking that seated actor and you can solve that easily using voms, aisles, or large set pieces. But start with the triangle and it will serve you well.

Next. Are you a director who prefers to sit at the tech table as you stage? It's okay if you are—but be sure to place that table in your rehearsal area in one of the smaller sections—ideally exactly opposite from the largest seating sections. I cannot tell you how many arena stagings I've seen that look like pure thrust with the smaller sections of the audience left to watch the show from what might as well be backstage. There's no question in my mind where the director sat throughout rehearsal—dead center in the largest section. It cheats the audience, certainly, but it also removes part of the amazing dynamic of arena staging.

Let's talk about set pieces (furniture) and placement. The last thing you want is a group of settees or divans, poufs, you name it, in a nice little inner circle around the stage following the line of the arena. Here's where directors and set designers can shine—you have dozens of interesting angles to play with, as long as you follow the basic rule of thumb: a seated actor should ideally have her back to an aisle or entrance, not a portion of the audience. And an actor facing a seated actor should not be blocking that stationary actor from the audience—a step or two right or left invariably opens that seated actor to the audience.

Of course not every show is a parlor piece. Arena sets may be full of platforming, cut-away walls, dividers, benches—all the same applies.

Now, you actors: directors come in all varieties; some come into staging with every cross, every motion already in their scripts. But you can become students of arena acting long before rehearsal starts if you have access to the space. Walk it. Find the sweet spots—you'll feel them as you stop, rotate, and appreciate the strength of your position; by the same token, you can locate those 'out of the way' positions for larger casts when your characters aren't holding focus. Mind you, this is the director's job, but most directors I know (including myself) truly appreciate actors with a sense of the space; I call them actors with three-dimensional brains. As I approach staging shows, unless a scene includes seven or eight (or more) actors, my preference is to allow the actors to explore their way through the scene without my interference; motivated blocking is invariably strongest. Then I step in to shape and create focus when necessary; but gifted actors comfortable in their space unafraid of making mistakes are my absolute favorites.

Once the show is staged—for better or worse—you actors have your blocking. Despair not—unless you're playing a quadriplegic, even seated, you can rotate back and forth in reaction to other characters' movements, thus opening yourselves to different sections of the audience. And now you learn to act with your backs—audiences rarely need to see your faces to understand your characters' opinions. An extended arm, fingers drumming on the back of a sofa speaks wonders.

Now let's talk movement—on proscenium stages, we've been taught to stand, step sideways to clear the end of the sofa and then take that cross up right. Throw that out the window. All bets are off. We're in the glorious world of open turns, exposing ourselves to the entire audience as we rise to cross to another section of the stage. It's an excellent way to establish focus and carry the audience along with you. Rarely, rarely, do I ask actors to make a straight cross anywhere—opting instead for a slight arc. It's just visually more interesting and accommodates the three-dimensional world of the play.

In arenas—or thrusts for that matter—diagonals are everything. Nothing is more boring than shows conceived and staged on a traditional x/y axis. Of course directors, designers and actors are limited by the design of the arenas themselves, but the very strongest line of focus in any arena (I might make the same argument for prosceniums) is the longest diagonal. It's one of those intangibles—I'm sure you've all seen it. Learn to use it.

In the same vein, speaking of long diagonals, try to remember that in the arena, actors having even fairly intimate conversations needn't be so close to each other with rare exceptions. It's a unique spatial thing—the audiences will shorten the distance in their minds.

Finally, let's talk a little more about those one on one conversations—to this day I laugh at experienced actors in early blocking who join on stage, shoulder to shoulder, cheating out just a little—perfect proscenium position. Um—no, guys. You can face each other, remember? Of course they must align themselves on the correct axis with voms or aisles at their backs, but none of this side by side stuff unless walking down the wedding aisle.

This only brushes the surface of the delights of working in arenas and/or thrusts (personally, I prefer full arenas). Once you've found a home in an arena, you'll be loathe to return to a proscenium.

Notes

1 Konstantin Stanislavski, *An Actor Prepares*. London: Routledge, 1989, p. 92.
2 Michael Chekhov, *To the Actor: On the Technique of Acting*. London: Routledge, 2002, p. 14.
3 Michael Chekhov, *Lessons for Teachers of His Acting Technique*. Ottawa: Dovehouse Editions, 2000, p. 15.
4 Chekhov, *To the Actor*, p. 143.
5 Chekhov, *To the Actor*, p. 142.

The Secret Garden by Marsha Norman. In the round production directed by David Metcalf, lighting design by Camille Holthaus, set design by Kirby Moore, costume design by Dwight Larsen. Theatre in the Round, Minneapolis, MN. Credit: Mark Hutchinson

Credit: drawing courtesy of Pablo Guerra-Monje

6

SHARING THE TREASURES

All theatre requires a measure of generosity from its actors. We need to give a performance. We do not begin our endeavors seeking to make a product to sell, but rather a gift to give. A gift that can reveal truth, can offer connection, can make meaning out of the world around us. NTS staging takes this ideology and not only embraces it, but also manifests it—in rich physical detail of each character's connection to themselves and to each other. Not only this, we must maintain a connection with the audience at all times while simultaneously maintaining a thorough embodiment of the character. In the proscenium setting, the connection to the audience is made by clearly physicalizing your intentions, objectives, obstacles and inner psychology. But what if only one-fourth of the audience could see those moments of revelation as they came? Then you are not telling the story to the majority of the audience. When a family member is about to have a breakdown, the other members of the family often see the warning signs. But each member of the family will see this breakdown differently. Not only do they perceive things differently, but they also share different moments with the member in trouble, and with each other. The story told in the arena setting is telling the same story through different sets of eyes. You must find ways to 'give the warning signs' to everyone in your audience, which is very different than just showing the whole audience the same sign once or twice. You must share the treasure of your discoveries equally throughout the audience.

Although you may give a gold doubloon here and a ruby necklace there, everyone must share in the bounty. Crafting how to use the discoveries you have made throughout the early rehearsal process is the work you must do in the later rehearsal process.

Exercise 6.1 The Refrain

Based on MC's Tool Psychological Gesture

What is your character's main objective? What are the obstacles they are facing? These next set of exercises help actors take their initial ideas about objective and obstacle and lace them physically throughout a scene and eventually, throughout a production. But more than that, these exercises offer opportunities for actors to discover objective and obstacles through explorations in the body.

Chekhov's iconic exercises, known as Psychological Gestures (PG), are one of the technique's most useful tools. PGs are the physical embodiment of objective or, rather, the objective is the intellectual understanding of the physical metaphor of the character:

> Each character onstage has one main desire, and one characteristic manner of fulfilling this desire. . . . We know that the desire of this character is the Will ("what"), and his manner of fulfilling it is its quality ("how"). Since the Psychological Gesture is composed of the Will permeated with its qualities, it can easily embrace the complete Psychology of the Character.[1]

The PG is a gesture, an archetypal gesture that is given a specific quality that helps to define it. These combined gestures (archetype prescribed by Chekhov and then specified with quality by the actor) are then used either veiled in a performance, or more commonly as tools to discover character and prepare for performance. In the following exercises, we look at PGs in relation to NTS performance and staging.

In terms of NTS work, where the physical metaphor of the actor's objective must play out over and over in different ways throughout the scene and play, using the idea of a song 'refrain' can be useful. It is not necessarily a momentary beat or transition, but a series of beats that depict a downfall born from elements that were there all along. What is your character's tragic flaw? How was it there from the very beginning? 'Refrain' takes the idea of the PG and offers an easy way to incorporate the tool into character-building work as well as performance preparation for an audience on all sides.

Coaching The Refrain

Based on Chekhov's Work on Psychological Gesture

Objective: To create gestures for use in performance (veiled) or as tools to discover character.

Coach Refrain I, the Archetype Warm Up:

- A good way to begin working with gesture is to have the ensemble move around the space and call out some archetypal personae (AP) and ask them to find a gesture for these personae as soon as they hear the prompt. If a person takes too long reacting to the prompt, point out to them that they may be filtering (looking for the right answer) and ask them to instead fulfill the first gesture that comes to their body. It doesn't matter if it makes sense to anyone else or even to them. Here are some examples of archetypal personae:

  - King
  - Slave
  - Hero
  - Queen
  - Mother
  - Lover
  - Villain
  - Seducer (or Cad if they know the word)
  - Temptress (allow gender to be specific so that actors try on both)
  - Orphan
  - Father
  - Mad Man
  - Crazy Lady
  - Witch
  - Monster
  - Feel free to add more!

(*continued*)

(continued)

Actors engaged in 'Refrain I'.
Credit: Gordon Wenzel

- Once they begin, encourage them to make full body gestures in tableau. They don't need to be moving but they need to extend through the whole body. The first gestures help actors to think in terms of archetypes free of qualities, so encourage them to examine the choices they make.
- Did you give us a nurturing mother—now can you give us a mother who may be nurturing or not or could be other things? These first exercises also encourage the actor to think expansively with their body and to incorporate the four brothers—feelings of ease, the whole, form and beauty:
  - *Form.* Ask the actors to go from one extreme of the body to the other in the gesture. If your gesture is an unfolding, start at the most folded, contracted place your body can be and then transition before reaching the end into the fully expanded gesture.
  - *Beauty.* Then sustain this ending moment for a few beats.
  - *The Whole.* Ask them not to rush, have a clear beginning, middle and end.
  - *Ease.* Ask actors to add some resistance to the movement but at the same time to notice and release any unnecessary tension in the body.

- Once they have run through a series of APs, discuss with them which archetypes looked similar on all the actors and which didn't. Then ask how this may correspond to the Jungian idea of universal unconscious (the idea that the human unconscious is filled with archetypes that have been created by the whole of humanity and/or society, not by the individual). Note also the very diverse interpretations and how that is okay too—giving rise to the instinctual kinesthetic response.
- Then ask if they gave their APs a value judgment (unintended quality). Good or bad. Note that you didn't give them a quality, and if they applied one, that this is not archetypal. A hero who kills one person to save others is not completely good. An evil dictator who cares about their children is not completely bad. These are exciting and complex descriptions of multifaceted characters, but we are not there yet. We are only looking for the *archetypal form* of the person before we layer story, either good or bad, onto them. If there were any AP that everyone had trouble keeping neutral, ask them to go back and try some of those APs again. Ask them to work to remain neutral in terms of a value judgment, but at the same time give the gestures a full physicality in tableau that extends through their whole body. When they have run through them, ask them what has changed.

Coach Refrain II, Finding your Character's Metaphor:

- With your ensemble, take one session to work through all of the following archetypal gestures. If you have not worked with gestures before, take it easy and make sure the participants work hard but do not hurt themselves.
- There should be resistance (you get out of this what you put in) but ask them to avoid tension in unrelated parts of their body. If you do not have *To The Actor* by Michael Chekhov (the main reference for Archetypal and Psychological Gesture that has pictures of the ideal full body gestures), it is okay to have them improvise each gesture (give me the biggest possible push) so long as they are being mindful of their own limitations and what their body can do.

(continued)

(*continued*)

- Ask them to:

  - Start from their IAC position.
  - Find the one full body gesture that embodies this arche-typal gesture.
  - There should be no value judgment to the gesture, it is nei-ther good nor bad, it just is.
  - The gesture should adhere to the rules of the four brothers:

    - It should have a clear beginning, middle and end. Beginning and end should be physical opposites (left to right or up to down, etc.). An equivalent would be the preparation for the action, the action and the aftermath (sustained release). The sustained release should last for a few beats at least.
    - It should have a sense of form (an attention to the whole body in space).
    - It should have a feeling of ease (a focus on the move-ment as satisfying/gratifying to perform in some way).
    - It should have a feeling of beauty (an attention trying different ways until that one that strikes you as most interesting/captivates the imagination is found—and then a sustained ending point).

  - Repeat the movement over and over until they feel is it the strongest representation of the gesture.

- With each gesture, when actors become comfortable with the physical movement, ask them to incorporate first their breath (inhale should begin the prep, exhale should be middle and end) and then their voices as an extension of the body.
- Ask them to use their deep diaphragmatic voices emanating from their abdomens and groins (the granny panties area). Urge them to sustain the last moment (just like the sustained release of the physicality) instead of abruptly ending in a glot-tal shock.
- Work each individual gesture for at least 3–5 minutes.

Notes on Gestures

Chekhov originally only had seven gestures, but NMCA offers additional gestures which have been useful for many actors. I include them here because they are very useful in practice:

1. Push	8. Tear
2. Pull	9. Penetrate
3. Throw	10. Reach
4. Drag	11. Expand
5. Smash	12. Contract
6. Lift	13. Wring
7. Gather	

Actors engaged in 'Refrain II/Archetypal Gesture'.
Credit: Gordon Wenzel

- Once you have worked through all of those, have one to five actors stand and demonstrate one of the archetypal gestures for you. They can all show at the same time. Then ask for a quality from the other actors. They can be more abstract at first. Here are some examples:

  - Cold
  - Hot
  - Damp
  - Sticky
  - Swishy

(continued)

(*continued*)

- Dry
- Hollow
- Feel free to add your own!

- Once you have gathered enough abstract qualities, now ask all five actors to add each quality as you call them out to their archetypal gesture: a cold push; a hot pull; a damp tear; a sticky gather, etc.
- Now introduce one character from the play or from one you are working on. Ask the actors to list of some emotional qualities of this character. Examples include:

  - Honest
  - Grieving
  - Heroic
  - Whiny
  - Arrogant
  - Cruel
  - Add your own as you see fit.

- Once you have gathered enough emotional qualities about one character, ask all the actors to add these emotional qualities to an AG they have explored: the cruel lift; the grieving throw; the heroic smash, etc.
- As you walk around observing the work, pick one actor who has created something resonant. Have the other actors stop and ask them to watch the one actor's image and ask themselves if they perceived a image or metaphor in what they have seen.
- Give them examples of other kinds of metaphors that have come out of AG/PG work:

  - She was tearing her heart out and throwing it away.
  - He was happy to destroy—smashing something joyfully.
  - She was lifting something to watch it fall.
  - Add more as you find them in your work or the work of your ensemble.

- Discuss how these might become objectives for the character. Psychological gesture is an archetypal gesture that has a quality (or more than one) added to it. This gesture is the physical manifestation of we call 'the objective.' But the intellectual objective can come later!

- Ask them to consider their characters and then ask them all to get up on their feet and move around the room (stopping to plant when they want to work on a PG) and play with at least three different archetypes that may fit their characters.

- Two of the AGs they explore should be opposites of each other—such as push and pull and one should be out of left field, for example push/pull/wring. Another way to think of it is your first choice, the opposite of your first choice and then something random.

Note: Giving them an assignment to try many different versions, including the opposite of their first choice is an active way to work against the intellect. Often times the opposite of their first choice, the one they never would have chosen intellectually or even tried, actually ends up being the one that provides the most interesting results.

- Once they find an archetype they like, they should work on attaching different qualities to the AG until they find one that is particularly interesting. They should then see if there is a further image or metaphor that resonates with them that originates from this PG and that will become their character's refrain. Examples include:

  - I want to smash his stupid face into the ground. (A smash with the quality of bitterness.)
  - My heart tears a little more every time she leaves. (A tear with the quality of softness.)
  - It's so hard to breathe when he isn't here. (A expand/contract with the quality of deep resistance.)

- They may find themselves drawn to more than one. These could be competing objectives or maybe objectives and obstacles. A character can have more than one refrain. When you have given them anywhere from 10 to 20 minutes to work on these on

(continued)

(*continued*)

their own, bring them back to show the group and discuss what they have found.

Coaching Refrain III, Finding Uses through Veiling:

- Once they have been introduced to AGs, PGs and have found their character's 'refrain/s,' ask the ensemble to begin moving around the space working with the PGs. This movement could mean stopping and planting to work an AG at full 7 in terms of energy and abstract movement, or using the PG in a more concentrated way at a 1 or 2 while continuing to move. You can be flexible with moving and or stillness, they don't have to adhere to a rule in the exploration.
- Using Chekhov's method of 'veiling', ask actors to expand and make their movements as big as they can possibly be while still maintaining the PG. Call this a 7. It can be abstract, grotesque or cartoonish but the PG must still have all the components in it.
- Now ask them to take their PG to a 5, so less abstract and more realistic than a 7 but more abstract than a 2.
- Then down have them go down to a 3 and a 1 etc. One should be hardly perceivable. It is not an outward PG but rather one that is happening continually on the inside. Or is communicated perhaps with a glance or a breath. A helpful catch phrase is 'Have the gesture just up and underneath everything you are doing' or 'Just behind the eyes. Smash with your breath. Gather

Actors engaged in 'Refrain/Psychological Gesture III'.
Credit: Gordon Wenzel

with your gaze.' And so on. Chekhov used the useful word 'Simmer'—have the PG simmering just below the surface.

- When actors are in 'simmer mode,' be sure to make them aware that the energy is simmering up and underneath their whole body, not just their face, eyes, torso. Have them practice the 'whole body simmer.'

- After you have moved them up and down the numbers so they get used to working in this way (one is film-like realism, perceivable in a close up, 7 is giant amphitheater) move on to a scene.

- Ask each actor to 'give' the refrain of their PG to every audience (each side) at least three times (3 x 4 = 12 times) throughout the scene.

- Ask them to experiment with having the gesture threaded realistically into the scene (a 1–3) all the way up to the extreme or abstract (8–10). Realistic smashes could be interpreted as the way something is said or a firm tapping of a pencil on a tabletop. Abstract (10) could just mean they are doing their PG fully in the middle of the scene during a high point in the action or it could realistically work into the way something is expressed deeply and powerfully through voice or action (this is a rehearsal technique, they won't use it in performance).

- Another variation is to have them do the whole scene while adding their PGs along the way at a 7—and then to repeat the exercise allowing the same PGs at the same moment at 1.

- Remind them to be safe with themselves, each other and their set/props but then watch to see what happens. Be sure to let them know what moments were most powerful and ask them what story they were telling each side. Did they favor one side? Ignore another? What can be done?

- Have them run it again to alleviate these problems if there is time. After one rehearsal in one scene, it is enough to ask the actors to keep the refrain (and its adjustments and levels) available for other scenes in the play. They can also play with multiple, competing, complementary and/or contrasting refrains complementing or battling one another within one character. Make sure to ask actors to reveal what they are working on with

(continued)

(continued)

> you so you can help or shift the quality if it doesn't match what you are looking for as a director.
> - End by having them consider (and share if there is time) how their refrains reveal themselves throughout the play and how the metaphors of each actor's objectives play out over and over in different ways, like a 'refrain' or the chorus of a song, throughout the story.

Exercise 6.2 Bubble

Based on MC's Tool Personal Atmosphere

Atmosphere is one of Chekhov's most useful tools for creating an ambiance onstage, creating the world of the play. When actors work together to create atmosphere, amazing things can happen for the audience: "Atmosphere deepens the perception of the spectator."[2] The audience is pulled in. When the tool is localized to one actor, it can be shorthand for actor's physicality that always tells the story from the character's viewpoint. Unrelated to mood or swaying emotional state, personal atmosphere creates the 'mini-world' of the character that is perceivable for the audience. This world is a fully sustained, fully realized, deeply clear rendering of a character point of view and why she/he makes the choices they make.

Coaching Bubble

Adapted from Chekhov's Work on Personal Atmosphere

Objective: To create a personal atmosphere or perceivable character environment onstage.

Coach:

- In this exercise, your actors are just reacting, not in character but as themselves.
- Have your actors move around the room until they are comfortable in their own body and space.

- When they are ready, ask them to imagine that there is a bubble around them, one which surrounds them all the time. Maybe it surrounds their whole body, maybe just their head, they can decide. Tell them that they can expand or shrink this bubble at any time as they explore.
- Now begin to fill their bubble. Tell them to kinesthetically react to the prompt you give them, or what their bubble is filled with. Instruct them that this is not a 'mood' bubble. They cannot leave the bubble behind when something new draws their attention. This bubble colors their whole world, their whole life. It colors the good days, the bad days and everything in between.
- Begin to give them different bubble fillers to play with. Flow easily back and forth from the abstract through the more constructed:

    - Sunshine
    - Boredom
    - Glitter
    - Hunger
    - Pudding
    - Water
    - Darkness
    - Constant chatter
    - Sand
    - Pieces of glass
    - Whispers
    - Egg shells
    - Feathers
    - A spotlight
    - Stars
    - Loneliness
    - Magic
    - Thirst
    - Puppies
    - Snakes
    - Feel free to add your own!

(continued)

(continued)

- As they move, instruct them not to intellectually attach a value judgment: darkness might be scary for some or comforting for others but it doesn't have to be anything. Ask them instead to just play with 'whatever shows up.'
- Encourage them also not to 'perform' for each other or you but rather to allow themselves to discover and be surprised by what appears.
- Give them permission to keep open within the bubble if nothing immediately appears or something strange appears in response to a prompt. Practicing non-judgment in response to their reactions will serve them well here.
- Ask them not only to keep moving around the room but also to try things like sitting down, standing up, saying a few sentences to someone, asking a question.
- Once they have run though many, ask them to pick one that really resonated with them or was fun to work with, ask them to return to it and then have them move through the room acting on each new prompt layer on top of what they are already doing:
  - Allow the bubble to filter everything that comes in or goes out.
  - Allow your character to be someone in . . . (this city, this high school, this university, etc.).
  - Allow your character to be having a bad day. Perhaps they got up late? Missed an appointment? Lost something they needed? Fought with someone?
  - Allow your character to be having a great day. Perhaps they had a nice surprise? Met with a good friend? Found something they have been looking for? Just made a new connection?
- Once they have played with one bubble, ask them to switch to a different bubble filter that is the opposite of the one they were working with. Then run through the list of prompt layers again.
- Take the ensemble back through possible good days and bad days. Consider tailoring the days and moments in the days to the place in which your ensemble is actually working in. Examples:
  - New York City. Just missed the express train! Now you have to take the local.

- High School. Failed that calculus test you thought you were ready for.
- University. Slept through that 8:30 class again. Now what?

- Once they have worked through the second filter, ask them to fill the bubble with something else—something that reminds them of their character. Once they have picked the bubble filter, ask them to play with it (sitting, standing, talking, asking, telling, etc.).
- Once they have worked with this bubble a little, ask them to visualize the play and have their characters move through each of the days and moments between the scenes. Give them time to do this, each on their own.
- When they have finished, allow them to get up in front of each other and pick one moment from the play (or implied by the play) that they can show their character in their bubble. Examples of moments from plays include:

  - Hedda Gabler, after she burned the manuscript—getting ready for bed by herself.
  - Juliet waiting for the nurse to return.
  - Romeo hiding below Juliet's window before she gets there.
  - Medea playing with her children the day before she will murder them.
  - Antigone walking with Jason on her way home, the night before she will give herself up to die.

- Once they have performed, ask those watching to see if they can guess what was in each actor's bubble. If they do guess correctly—great, if they don't guess, that's okay too. Let actors know that sometimes, in order for the actor to find what they need to make the character resonate in a powerful way to the audience, they have to find a 'secret' image. What they find doesn't have to be strictly transparent to the audience. The energy, not the exact image, is what needs to be clear to the audience.
- Be sure to discuss what you as a facilitator saw as well and what is working or resonant for you as the director or teacher.

(continued)

(*continued*)

> If something was too blatant, you can always work with a veil-ing exercise to pull atmosphere more inward. Vice versa if you would like them to be more visible to an audience. Example:
>
> • Ask all the actors to stand and work on their character bub-bles and then take them through the numbers 1–7 in ran-dom order.
>
> • Then, as you work the scene work, ask them to bring the bubble into the scene and if you want more, ask them to reveal the energy of the bubble at a higher level. (You seem to be at a 2 or 3 here, reveal at a 4. 6. 7!) Call these num-bers out during the scene and make sure the actors know to keep playing through while you coach. You can even go back and forth—3, 5, 2, 7!
>
> • If you want them to be more realistic, consider the same exercise in the other direction: ask them to reveal the energy of the bubble at a lower level. (You seem to be at a 6 or 7 here, reveal at a 3. 2. 1!) If they are working on subtlety, make sure you encourage them to keep the energy level the same underneath—just to change the level at which they reveal this energy to the audience. That way your perfor-mances will always be exciting—'simmering' up and under-neath. Also, as before, encourage simmering with the whole body for a whole body/360 degree performance.

Exercise 6.3 Character Gestures and Jewelry: Vary the Repetition

Based on MC's Tools Psychological Gesture and Jewelry

As we move forward from creating the PGs and populating the imag-inary worlds of the personal atmospheres, we can begin to add what Chekhov once described to Mala Powers as Improvisational Jewelry: "Rehearsing invented activities will make it easier to develop the 'jewelry' in your performances—nuances and little shining moments of uniqueness that are memorable and that delight both you and the audience."[3] In this next exercise, Wil Kilroy offers improvisations from which to mine buried gestural treasures of all sorts that may be fun and delightful when used to adorn your character.

Coaching Character Gestures and Jewelry

Based on Chekhov's Ideas of Gesture and Jewelry

By Wil Kilroy

Objective: To discover broad categories of gesture and to be facile with interweaving them so as not to become repetitive with personal, habitual movements but to instead discover innovative gestures for the character.

Coach:

- Actors divide into teams.
- The first task is to direct each other to a nearby location, thereby using indicative gestures—pointing to and referencing landmarks along the way. This should also result in turning and moving in the space to further enhance comfort presenting at all angles.
- For the next task, the team will focus on illustrating gestures—which might be actually showing how a certain recipe is made, or depicting in the air favorite holiday decorations.
- Third, the team should talk to each other about something that they are very passionate about—perhaps politics, making definitive points accenting them with emphatic gestures—perhaps a fist slamming into the palm or a foot stomp or palms pressing forward.
- The last topic could simply be about the weather, but each actor finds habitual gestures that can be commonly observed—tossing the hair back, scratching, stroking the chin, playing with a corner of clothing. Again, they explore this with the team.
- After these four categories (indicating gestures, illustrating gestures, passionately emphatic gestures, habitual gestures) are experienced, an improvisation can be created.

(continued)

(*continued*)

- You as the facilitator can assign arbitrary characters, location and what's happening or the group can.
- As the actors run through the scene, call out a type of gesture and actors must immediately focus on using that kind of gesture to accomplish the objective in the scene.
- Variation: assign one person to call out gestures to each actor in the scene and have them work simultaneously.
- After the improv has played for a while, allow the calling to stop and encourage the actor to continue to find variation of gesture by presenting a mixture of the categories.
- When moving into scene work, you can run this whole exercise again, but as the characters that the actors are working with.

Another fun way of improvising using Wil's technique is to ask actors to begin this exercise by writing a list of 'deleted scenes' from the play or from their character's history that they would like to see. Use that list to create improvs that build character memories and background while simultaneously exploring gesture. The deleted scenes sometimes offer great insight into why the characters make the choices they do within the play. The gestures then become twice as meaningful to the actors and palpably more important to the audience.

Exercise 6.4 Music as Character: Your Inner Monologue

Inspired by MC's Ideas on Active Analysis

According to Chekhov:

Of course the actor must know everything he possibly can. But the difference is in how he knows it . . . The cold intellect is the kind in which we do not see anything but facts. But if our knowledge is at the same time an imaginative picture then everything is alright . . . the intellect (should be) in the position of a servant who carries a candle and does nothing but throws light.[4]

In this exercise, Wil Kilroy asks the actors do their homework and instead of writing down a character analysis or a character bio (employing the cold intellect only), he asks them to find the internal music of their character. Preferably several pieces of music, a playlist. Encourage actors not to be too precious with their choices, they don't have to be perfect matches, just interesting possibilities. Once the playlist is created, ask actors to bring them into rehearsal, play them (they can skip ahead after a taste of each song) and then continue with the following exercise.

Coaching Music as Character

Based on Chekhov's Ideas on Active Analysis

By Wil Kilroy

Objective: To utilize inner music for character development.

Coach:

- You may recall the movement exercise to real and imagined music from Chapter 5, which allowed for actors to break out of their comfort zone via the inspiration of diverse musical selections.
- For this exercise the actor now chooses a piece of music to be played inside their head as an inner monologue.
- This is done in conjunction with either an improvisation which has a set scenario to explore, or could be done with a memorized scene, allowing the musical choice to influence character expression from movement to vocal dynamic.
- Results should be very different if the inner music begins as a sappy ballad and then moves into hard rock.
- After the scene is completed, observers can give feedback to the actors about what the results were: what type of character did they witness, what emotional states seemed to be present and what was their relationship to their partner. What is communicated to the audience is much more important that what was chosen musically for the inner monologue.

This exercise can be done with or without sharing the music or the playlist. But when shared, it is interesting to watch where changes from one song to another may occur internally and actors can give each other strong feedback on what the audience receives from what the actor is sending out and 'playing' underneath.

Exercise 6.5 Tornado: Activating Personal Atmosphere through the Body and Voice

Based on MC's Tool Personal Atmosphere

Working with the ideas from Exercise 6.2 'Bubble', which focuses on Chekhov's explorations of personal atmosphere, here Samantha Norton offers an excellent vocal and physical warm-up that introduces a set internal atmosphere to work with, and one that can give actors the sensation of a full body experience.

Coaching Tornado

Based on Chekhov's Ideas on Personal Atmosphere

By Samantha Norton

This all-encompassing exercise complements Chekhov's concept of Personal Atmosphere with a touch of understanding what 'Radiating' can feel like!

Objective: At the end of the Tornado exercise, your students will experience expansiveness in their breath, voice and movement—free of physical/psychological restriction.

Coach the Tornado Prep:

- To begin, have everyone lie on the floor, eyes closed, with enough space between to roll about and swing their arms. If space is limited, you'll ask your students to open their eyes when they become more physical.
- As their instructor, let your students know that the exercise will take 5, 10 or 15 minutes, depending on your time (this keeps you and them from rushing or anticipating the next step).

Coach Tornado Meditation:

- Share with the actors:

  - You have been told that a Tornado is soon to come your way. You do not need to run because you know the storm will not harm you. Instead, you anticipate its arrival.
  - Begin by observing your calm, easy breath. With your eyes closed, notice to your right or left a small dark cloud. You can barely see it, but you notice it spinning.
  - Now, place that tiny spinning image inside your belly button. Imagine it starting to spin inside you, very small and almost invisible at first. Add your breath to this image. Now let your breath and imagination allow the Tornado to start spinning out to your ribs and back. Start to feel your torso move in sync with your 'spinning' breath.
  - Your stomach is becoming more engaged and the breath is stronger. Once you feel you have the Tornado filling your chest and back, allow the arms, legs and head to be activated by the rhythm of the breath a bit more.
  - Keep the image of the Tornado filling your body all the way out to your fingers, toes, neck and top of your head. By now your body and breath are moving faster.
  - Soon the momentum of the breath and movement will take your body to one side or the other and eventually up to standing (eyes open if it's a crowded space).
  - Once you find yourself standing, keep moving the body in any direction the Tornado may take you. It doesn't have to be spinning, you can move in any direction your breath takes you. (This is the biggest part of the Tornado!)
  - Keep breathing and moving up to the point where you feel the storm has reached its peak inside you.
  - Now, begin to slowly, with your breath and movement, let the Tornado get smaller; taking it all the way back to you finding yourself on the floor where the storm shrinks back into a tiny dot in your belly button.
  - On one final exhale, blow that tiny dot away.

I also find Sam's exercise is just as effective if students remain on the floor with eyes closed as opposed to standing and moving at the height of the exercise. Both variations can result in strong physical expansiveness after the exercise is completed as well an opening up of the breath and voice, should the actor and facilitator choose to explore vocally during the meditation. This exercise also leaves actors with a strong physical sense of how vibration and movement resonates through the body.

Advice from the Pros: Costuming in the Round—A Question of Your Point of View

By Sue Picinich

Costumes must be pretty much the same in the round as in any other type of staging, right? Well, as with many things, the answer is yes and no. In all staging—proscenium, thrust or in the round—the actors turn and move so costumes are viewed from all angles. Some seats are close and some are at the back of the house so costumes are

Susan Picinich, costume designer.
Credit: Sue Picinich

viewed at various distances. Actors appear in front of a variety of backgrounds—from curtains to solid-looking walls to painted back-drops. And in every kind of theatre, the lighting can change color, angle and brightness. So what's special about theatre in the round?

In my experience as a professional and academic costume designer, I think the significant differences stem from the point of view of the audience. I designed regularly at North Shore Music Theatre in Beverly, Massachusetts, which is an 1800-seat theatre in the round, also known as an arena theatre. The closest seats are so close that the audience members can reach out and touch the stage, and even the last row is only 10 rows from the first.

While working there, I encountered three major considerations related to this theatre configuration:

- Distance between audience and performers.
- Background behind the performers.
- Physical characteristics or layout of actors' entrances and backstage.

Let's consider each of these using North Shore Music Theatre examples.

Distance to Performers

With musicals produced in a proscenium theatre, there is usually a rela-tively wide space—often including an orchestra pit—between the front row and the stage. Also, the stage is usually elevated above the audience.

The Full Monty finale at North Shore Music Theatre 2005. Costume design by Susan Picinich.

Credit: Susan Picinich

In the round, actors can be much closer and the stage may be level with the front row. In musical theatre this means that wig lace, mic packs, underdressing for quick changes, and other tricks of the trade can be examined and scrutinized in more than usual detail. It also means that rented costumes, often used for time-and-cost saving in regional musical theatre, which were originally designed for large proscenium theatres, are on view as if under a microscope. I clearly recall encountering this issue while costuming *A Little Night Music* at North Shore in 2000. In "Every Day a Little Death," the actresses playing Charlotte and Anne sat on a bench right at the edge of the stage. The fit of Charlotte's gown and the tilt of her hat caused me major consternation until we had everything perfect for up-close viewing as well as sightlines around her brim for the back row. This proximity to the audience has come into play frequently over the years, requiring finesse and refinement beyond that called for in larger venues.

Background

In arena staging, the costumes are often the most prominent design element. To allow clear sightlines, there is usually little scenery and no backdrops or stage curtains to help set the scene. Costumes need to provide most of the usual expected information about period, location, character and mood. But they also need to 'pop' even when you can see the faces and figures of other audience members across the theatre in the background. The view of the audience members across the way became a big factor in the 2005–6 season production of *The Full Monty*. The finale relies on a staging trick (spoiler alert) which casts the male 'strippers' into a backlit silhouette. In the North Shore Music Theatre version, the actors stood in an outward facing circle as they doffed their policeman hats. Bright lights did indeed create the silhouette effect. But viewers also got a brief and surprising glimpse of the bare back view across the circle before lights out. This view included the surprised expressions of their fellow playgoers. In the blackout the actors exited via an automated lift center stage and they reentered for their curtain call (covered up in bathrobes) the same way. Maybe this was a fun extra provided by arena staging. It was certainly different.

Physical Layout

Theatre in the round creates special challenges and opportunities because of the physical layout of the space, especially the location of entrances and exits for the performers. Rather than quickly ducking behind a flat, a curtain or the proscenium, actors often exit up the aisle through the audience. For costumes this can mean more than usual walking or running in full view of the audience. Such movement can be awkward in period or specialty costumes—consider the crocodile in Peter Pan or any lady in a hoop skirt. The designer also needs to be sure large costumes will fit through the aisle, and plan for added time to get to whatever area is serving as 'backstage.' Musicals such as *Les Miserables* are sung-through, which means the music and therefore the action is continuous. The timing of the many required quick-changes needs to include some significant travel time to get out of sight. Also the potential quick-change locations are limited in an arena theatre. At North Shore we had temporary quick-change booths in the house behind the last row of seats and in the lobby. This required very quiet and low-light costume changes. Other quick-change locations may be under the stage, accessed by a vomitorium (passage beneath the seats) or a lift. Both are useful for getting actors and large props to the acting area. But lifts also create timing challenges, since they never run as fast as you want. Another layout consideration is that there is no direction which can be considered as upstage in the round. Some audience member in the theatre is directly in front of or behind every bit of the action. Actors and costumers do not have an opportunity to conceal stage business by turning away. This cuts out some tried and true tricks while opening the door to creative new staging. The *Full Monty* finale remains my best example of a unique consequence of arena staging. The entire company collaborated to come up with an artistically viable solution to the expected reveal, and the actors were very good sports as we worked through the ending in tech.

The End Result

In the end, designing costumes for an arena theatre does not require any extraordinary adaptations of the regular design process. In fact, working in a different physical environment can help you see your

costumes and your process with fresh eyes. The point of view of the
theatre artists creating work in the round is also influenced by the
choice of staging. This renewed perspective is a boon to designers, as
it puts you in line with audience members who are encountering your
work for the first time. For costumes in the round you should especially consider the closeness of the viewers, the background and how
the logistics of the stage layout contributes to the audience's experience of the production. With these points in mind, costumes in the
round are a regular device in the designer's toolkit.

Notes

1 Michael Chekhov, *On the Technique of Acting*. New York: Harper, 1993,
  p. 90.
2 Michael Chekhov, *To the Actor: On the Technique of Acting*. London: Routledge,
  2002, p. 48.
3 Chekhov, *On the Technique of Acting*, p. xlii.
4 Chekhov, *Lessons for Teachers of His Acting Technique*. Ottawa: Dovehouse
  Editions, 2000, p. 38.

Rosencrantz and Guildenstern are Dead by Tom Stoppard. In the round production directed by John Gaspard, lighting design by Peter W. Mitchell, costume design by Rebecca Ballas, scenic design by Chad Van Kekerix. Theatre in the Round, MN. 2010.

Credit: Theatre in the Round, Minneapolis, MN

Credit: drawing courtesy of Pablo Guerra-Monje

7

ENTERING THE EXPERIENCE

In the round staging is in many ways more intimate, more experiential for the audience than traditional Western proscenium staging. The audience can see not only the actors performing on stage, but also the other audience members who are seated across. They are watching the story unfold and other audience members' experience of the story and that becomes a part of the performance. The actors too can see the audience in a much more visceral way. The audience is often visible, because in many theatres they can never be fully in the dark when lights from the stage spill out in every direction. Actors who are used to performing 'out' find themselves, instead, seeking to pull the audience 'in.' Seeing the audience not as a distraction from the performance but as integral to the experience of the performance can be a very exciting proposition for the actor.

In this way, the audience becomes a character in the play, another player with whom actors must establish trust, connection and shared energy. Non-traditional stagings of productions often become less about repeating exact blocking and more about repeating an experience between scene partners, like a moment in history repeating itself with tiny variations depending on the audience/time traveller whose gaze changes the picture through the sheer active act of watching. Akin to the merging exercises of Chapter 5 (5.3 The Matrix), the audience is asked to partake in the experience of the communal story by sending and receiving energy, just as the actors do and then to merge with the thing they are focused on, the play. This is not a passive movie theatre type of experience. This is a campfire ghost story experience. We are all telling/getting scared/excited together. And the scary part is that the ghost, murder, etc. could be out there in the woods, behind us all. In the best of stories, the ones that tell the truth, the ghost is real, even if the story is not.

Pablo Picasso called art 'the lie that tells the truth.' And theatre is one of the last places in our Western society where sharing truths about who we are as humans is the most important goal. So how do we approach, prepare for this kind of experience as the performers, creators of the story? When creating a communal event, often times the answer is ritual. We are used to ritual being a large part of communal events at places such as churches, temples, mosques and other religious gathering spaces. Rituals are also a part of sports, concerts, traditional Western theatre. Theatre artists have been very interested in ritual throughout time, owing to so much of traditional Eastern and Western theatre began intertwined with religion and the sacred. Chekhov often referred to this kind of work as 'baptizing' the text, space, play, character. Starting a rehearsal for an non-traditional staging can benefit from a few specific ritual/exercises that ask the performers to invest, from the beginning, in something bigger than their part of the story alone. Communal cast rituals/exercises can not only reinforce the ensemble feeling of the group, but also prepare them to invite the audience in, in a deeper more visceral way once the show is running.

Exercise 7.1 The Helpers

Based on MC's Tools Concentration,
Receiving/Radiating and Merging

A few years ago, a story circulated around the Internet. It was about Fred Rogers (from PBS's *Mister Rogers* in the 1960s, 1970s and 1980s) and a short essay he wrote about how his mother helped him when he was little to deal with difficult things in the news. He told this story most of his life, but the story would often recirculate widely again just following a tragic event: 9/11, Columbine, Sandy Hook, Katrina, the attacks in Paris, Pakistan, etc. It is now on the PBS site on their 'Helping Children with Scary News' page. Here is the story:

Fred Rogers often told this story about when he was a boy and would see scary things on the news: "My mother would say to me, 'Look for the helpers. You will always find people who are helping.' To this day, especially in times of 'disaster,' I remember my mother's words, and I am always comforted by realizing that there are still so many helpers—so many caring people in this world."

This ritual helps the actor establish ways to find their anchors in performance, the ones that will help them through the good performances and through the bad. Through the difficult times and the easy times. Finding the helpers is a way to keep the cast in control of the story and their own emotional investment in the performance no matter what happens. And in theatre, where live performance is often fraught with the pitfalls (and the glories) of 'anything can happen' these small life preservers can be the unsung heroes of the show.

Coaching The Helpers

Based on Chekhov's Ideas of Concentration, Receiving/Radiating and Merging

Objective: To give an ensemble a way to keep control of their own emotional investment in the performance no matter what happens.

Coach:

- Have your ensemble move around the space. If you are in a rehearsal hall, it is fine to establish the practice there so long as you also devote a little time to the same exercise once you get in the space with the actual set.
- Ask them to look around the space as if they are entering into it for the first time, like an audience member who has never been to the theatre, but is looking forward to it.
- As they move around this space, ask them to notice small details about the space and the architecture, and when they find something particularly interesting, to stop and spend some

(continued)

(*continued*)

time with it. They may touch the detail, smell, etc. They are not merging as before, but rather, *befriending* the detail.

- Ask them to consciously give these details personalities. It is possible that you may get one or two folks who find anthropomorphizing small elements of the theatre is silly. If you have such folks, ask them to instead imagine the people who raised the money for the theatre and built this space and what their greatest hopes for the space were, then attach these imagined figures to each of the details or spaces they find.

- Have your ensemble imagine artists/actors that came before them, especially the ones that had a great love for what they did in this place or maybe who persevered against difficult challenges to be there. We'll call these people 'ghosts.' Ask them to become aware of the 'ghosts' within the space.

- After a minute or two, ask them to find another detail, perhaps one even more welcoming and 'friendly' than the first. Those imagining people of the past should imagine a new person/ghost, in a new part of the theatre, showing them something else.

- Once the cast has gotten three to four details or 'spots' situated around the space, ask them again to walk around the space imagining or thinking about their part in the upcoming the play. Imagine a good night of performance.

- Ask them to take in one of their spots and imagine there is support coming from that element/detail/spot/ghost. Ask them to walk around again and imagine an off night in performance. Have them find one of the spots and ask them to once again feel the support that is coming from there. Then to use that support to move forward.

- Now ask the cast to imagine audience all around them, on all four sides. Pick out a chair and imagine a person there who is excited and 'into' the play. Alternatively, they could anthropomorphize a friendly chair as well. Ask them, just as before, to spend some time with each audience spot. They need to do this on all four sides.

- When they are finished, ask them once again to move around the stage running through the play or scenes from the play in their mind. Ask them to check in with their spots, details, audience members or ghosts as needed. They do not need to look directly at a spot to know it's sending energy and support, although they could, in soft focus, at an important part of the play if they like.

- Once they have gotten comfortable with that, ask them to imagine a new night and a full audience. The audience members from before are no longer there, but are replaced with new ones. As they move around the space, ask them to imagine performing but with an expanded sense of awareness, ask them to find their helpers, the ones who are so involved in the play that they are sending energy and support to you from their seat. Ask the cast not to look directly at these people, but to instead feel the energy and let it support and grow their work on stage. Ask them to imagine one of their best nights and the feeling of support from many people on all sides.

- Once you have run this set of exercises, allow there to be some discussion and reaction. Note in particular any places where actors found support, peace of mind and/or positive energy from unexpected places. Discuss the long legacy of your play, your theatre, actors who have come before you, the theatre itself. Now have your ensemble imagine actors playing their roles years from now. Imagine those actors imagining this ensemble, then ask them what they would want to say if they were the ghosts in the audience. Let these ideas sink in a bit.

- At the next few rehearsals, and/or added as a warm-up once you get to performances, have the actors check in with positive details/spots and ghosts in the theatre. Ask them to find these helpers every night. In addition, once the show is on its feet, tell your actors to keep their antennae open to the real audience and look for those new helpers night to night. There will always be those who are drifting, sleeping, bored or out of it. Don't let them suck up your energy! Find the helpers. Sometimes, they are all you need to give your best performance.

Exercise 7.2 The Revelation Spell

Inspired by MC's Ideas on the Higher Ego and Ensemble

When I was 19 years old I watched a movie called *The Bad Lieutenant* with Harvey Keitel. It was an excellent movie, acted well with a strong story line. It was however, a bit too much for me. The story was about a young nun that was raped by a group of young local boys whose poverty and dire circumstances had led them to act out in an unconscionable way. They were regretful but the community was filled with rage, wanted them to go to jail and maybe get the death penalty. When questioning the nun, she replied she had already forgiven them. After the lieutenant had found out much more about the terrible circumstances of the boys, he was torn, he hated what the boys did but felt if only they had been raised in different circumstances perhaps things would have been different. In the end, instead of arresting the boys, he put them on a bus to leave town. After the movie I was furious, I hated the movie! Those boys should have gone to jail. For years afterwards I hated the movie. Yet slowly, as I got older, I began to understand that the movie was about forgiveness—the most difficult painful kind of forgiveness that was such a big part of human experience and a religious life. I hated the movie when I saw it, but years later I saw it for a brilliant piece of art dealing with the great potential and capacity of the human heart. Yet at that moment, right when I saw it, I was not in a place to see that then. I couldn't. I wouldn't. I needed time, years to process and fully come to terms with that story.

As a professor, I occasionally come across students who hate some form, style or methodology that I am teaching. Often times so passionately that, when I was a young professor, I would feel hurt by the rejection of something I felt so passionate about. Yet time and again I meet those students 5, 10 even 20 years later who tell me that they no longer feel the same way about the work. That something in them has changed and that they are now so grateful for the lessons they initially learned with me then. Sometimes they even apologize professing, "Jeez, I was kinda a pain in the butt there for a while wasn't I?" I am not saying this is always the case, but often it is. In performance whether we are teaching, learning or experiencing it as an audience, there is often a time-release component that we cannot account for. Some film and theatre is easily digestible, but other pieces take more time, some even more than we will ever know or get to see. Sometimes the person who observed the piece is changed by the piece. As artists, that is our greatest hope. The danger is in expecting that to happen immediately or overnight. People need time to sit with big ideas, sometimes they need to get a little older or gather more experience before it can resonate authentically for them. As actors, we tend to lean into the expectation of a certain immediate response.

In arena staging, where the response is so much more present because actors can often see the audience up close, we run the danger of reading into a person's reactions. Seeing a person not laugh, not cry or not respond in the way that you hoped can sabotage an actor's performance if he/she lets it. What if they laugh when they should be crying? Or not laugh when the punch line is delivered? Actors will often believe that either the audience is not with them or, worse, that their performance is somehow lacking, both of which can often lead to a less brave performance that is still happening, either that night or into the run. Sometimes the audience is digesting the performance and they may need time to do it. The goal is to let go of your expectations and just give the same gift every night. If they are with you, wonderful, but if you aren't feeling it the same way, allow that it is hitting them differently and that is not only okay, but it could also be better in the long run. Theatre is transitory, but stories can last in people's minds as long as they live. Allow for that gift to have its due.

But what if a person looks out and out bored? That's very different than time release. My thought here is that yes sometimes plays can be boring to some and not to others, so keep giving the gift to those who are still with you. Do not let the one person checking their watch or texting ruin your gift for the one person in the back who really needs this show, who is having a deep personal reaction. Keep giving. There is also the chance that you are not the best audience reader in the world. Ever have the experience of thinking the show was an 'off night' only to have a stranger tell you it was one of the best shows they'd ever seen? I have. You will. Just because they are quiet or hidden or out and out not responding or laughing the way you think they ought to does not mean they are not with you. Sometimes you can know and sometimes you cannot know. You must keep giving everything you've got all the same. There are also those who respond differently because they might be neuroatypical—audience members who might process information differently, who may not look at something the way most people do, or react the way that most people do in the moments you would like them to. From people on the Autism Spectrum to those with ADHD, Dyspraxia, Dyslexia—there are many different ways to be and to respond to performance. Honor your neurodiverse audience with allowing them to have genuine responses that might be different from everyone else. Honor them by giving them the same gift.

I am not saying there is no such thing as a bad performance or a boring show. That is an issue for a director to surmise after previews or after the show has ended. What I am saying is more often than not, actors are more willing to believe their show or their own performance is flawed when not receiving the response they expect and they allow this problematic interpretation of the information to influence the rest of their performance negatively. Your job is not to assess audience response. Your job is to give your performance to the best of your ability every night.

The essence of our profession is to give. What is it that we in the theatre give? We give our body, voice, feelings, will, imagination—we give a form of pulsating art to life itself; we give it to our characters and we give it to our audiences. Nothing, absolutely nothing remains for us save the pleasure of having given pleasure. And yet it is only by this miraculous process that our love grows and our talent is fulfilled and replenished.

The next exercise is an ensemble-led ritual building tool. Creating the ensembles 'revelation spell' relies on the theory that words have power. The word 'spell' can also be seen as an affirmation, a way to reaffirm and remind the group that the performance is bigger than any one small perception of approval or disapproval. It creates a mission statement of sorts that initiates a call to our Greater Creative Individuality—our individual distinct voices that can only be attained in service to the Higher Ego. Chekhov said:

> Our artistic natures have two aspects: one that is merely sufficient for our ordinary existence and another of a higher order that marshals the creative powers in us. By accepting the objective world of the imagination, the independent interplay of our images, and the depth of the subconscious activity of our creative lives, we open up the very limited boundaries of our "personalities." We confront the Higher Ego.[1]

The Revelation Spell opens an ensemble's connection to the Higher Ego:

> This longing for knowledge makes the real artist brave. He never adheres to the first image that appears to him, because he knows that this is not necessarily the richest and most correct. He sacrifices one image for another more intense and expressive, and he does this repeatedly until new and unknown visions strike him with their revealing spell.[2]

Chekhov believed the magical power of story and imagery was akin to a spell that actors, like sorcerers, could invoke with the skill of their artistry and commitment. This spell revealed to the actor truths about her/his character, the play—about humanity and human nature as a whole. This exercise asks the actors to see themselves as artist/conjurers invoking a revelation spell for themselves and for the audience.

Coaching The Revelation Spell

Inspired by Chekhov's Ideas on the Higher Ego and Ensemble

Objective: A way for actors to invest in truths that are revealed through the performance of the play.

Coach:

- Ask your actors to sit in a circle around the stage facing in toward each other. Hand out this list of quotes or other quotes you are interested in, and feel free to add more to them. Have each actor read one out loud that resonates with him/her. Once around the circle, begin a discussion about story and how or why it is important. Once the discussion peaks, ask actors in groups of two or three to take a few quotes and turn them into affirmations or 'spells.' Here is are examples:

  Quote: "If stories come to you, care for them. And learn to give them away where they are needed.

  (continued)

(*continued*)

> Sometimes a person needs a story more than food to stay
> alive."—Barry Lopez (as Badger, in *Crow and Weasel*)
>   *Spell:* "We care for this story. We give away this story.
> Someone in this world needs this story more than food.
> Someone is here tonight."

Or

> *Quote:* "Fairy tales are more than true: not because they
> tell us that dragons exist, but because they tell us that
> dragons can be beaten."—G.K. Chesterton
>   *Quote:* "Lies to reveal the truth."—Stella Adler
>   *Spell:* "This story is more than true, it is a lie that reveals
> what is true. Our characters exist only through us, in order
> to reveal what is true."

- Once your actors have their affirmations/spells, have them once again circle up and share what they have created.
- Pick three of these spells and write them on a board, piece of butcher paper or somewhere else where everyone can see them.
- Once that is done, speak to your actors about audience response. Include a discussion on time-release response and/ or neurodiversity. Then ask each actor to gently amend their spells if they choose to. For example: "Someone in the audience needs this story more than food—even if they don't know it yet."
- Give them 2–5 minutes to create or amend one on their own, if they need amending, and then share them one by one.
- As a group, select which one is most meaningful to the group. Now add that spell to the others to make four that everyone can see. Then have your actors repeat them. Then have them stand and repeat them. Then have them look out into the audience and repeat them.
- Ask them which spells felt most meaningful inward to the group and which felt most meaningful outward towards the audience.
- Perhaps then pick two toward the group and two toward the audience.
- Lastly, ask your actors to pick another that is meaningful to just them. That one they will begin with. Once that is established,

tell your actors that you have created a revelation spell for the ensemble and the audience.

- Say this spell at the end of warm-ups before every performance to remind actors why they are doing what they are doing what is important and what they intend to do for the audience. For example:

1. End of Warm Ups
2. Revelation Spell:

    a. Everyone stands in a circle, actors whisper the first affirmation (their personal one) to themselves.

    b. Everyone stands in a circle, actors say the second affirmation (from story quote) out loud to each other.

    c. Everyone stands in a circle, actors say the third affirmation (from story quote) out loud to each other or where the audience will be.

    d. Everyone stands in a circle, actors say the fourth affirmation (from story quote) out loud to where the audience will be.

    e. Everyone stands in a circle, actors say the fifth affirmation (created from the group) out loud to (you decide) the bigger audience, theatre, world, God and beyond.

Note: These levels of who the actors are speaking to match the Circles of Focus, as described in the Coaching Focal Points exercise from Chapter 4: first circle is personal, second circle is to another person, third circle is to the people in the room, fourth is to the crowd or the audience, fifth is to God or the powers that be. Alternatively you can also use the fourth as referring to as God and the fifth is memory. Or vice versa. Really, it is up to you so long as you are consistent and specific.

Other Potential Quotes for Spells

People think that stories are shaped by people. In fact it's the other way around.

—Terry Pratchett

(*continued*)

(*continued*)

There have been great societies that did not use the wheel, but there have been no societies that did not tell stories.

—Ursula K. LeGuin

If stories come to you, care for them. And learn to give them away where they are needed. Sometimes a person needs a story more than food to stay alive.

—Barry Lopez
(as Badger, in *Crow and Weasel*)

Story is the vehicle we use to make sense of our lives in a world that often defies logic.

—Jim Trelease

Of course it's true, but it may not have happened.

—Patricia Polacco's grandmother

Lies to reveal the truth.

—Stella Adler

God made man because he loves stories.

—Rabbi Nachman of Bratzlev
(as quoted by Steve Sanfield)

The destiny of the world is determined less by the battles that are lost and won than by the stories it loves and believes in.

—Harold Goddard
(*The Meaning of Shakespeare*)

Fairy tales are more than true: not because they tell us that dragons exist, but because they tell us that dragons can be beaten.

—G.K. Chesterton

> Australian Aborigines say that the big stories—the stories worth telling and retelling, the ones in which you may find the meaning of your life—are forever stalking the right teller, sniffing and tracking like predators hunting their prey in the bush.
>
> —Robert Moss, Dreamgates

- Feel free to find other quotes to use in this exercise.

Exercise 7.3 Gifts

Inspired by MC's Ideas on Artistic Individuality, Jewelry and Beauty

I once had a director who would ask us to 'bring her gifts' every rehearsal. For her, gifts were new choices on moments and beats. We did not always appreciate this request for gifts without a clear direction or even some guidelines on what sort of gifts would be appreciated. Certainly this ask was something she considered a great gift to us, the ability to be intimately connected with the choices made about the character instead of just having to heed a director's concept. The invitation to collaborate was indeed a wonderful gift, but we were too young and inexperienced to appreciate it. We needed better tools with which to form our ideas. It was hard for us to find new ways to interpret our characters without some kind of inspiration. A muse. An idea. An image. The next exercise is a way for the entire cast to be complicit in the collaboration of each individual's character through a set of gifts, continued gifts that can be given throughout the process. They are little inspirations that the actor can choose to act on, use for their own purposes in creating/interpreting character objective, physicality, mask, trajectory, etc. The last set of gifts reminds the ensemble about their dedication to each other and to the play.

Coaching Gifts

Based on Chekhov's Ideas of Artistic Individuality,
Beauty and Jewelry

Objective: A way for the ensemble to offer individual actors little bits of inspiration about their characters, which they can use or discard as they see fit.

Coaching Gifts 1, Drawing Down the Play:

- Have your actors find a comfortable spot on the floor, sitting or lying down, and close their eyes. After a little time deep breathing or performing a meditation (like Mind Sweat in Chapter 5), ask them to just let their breathing fall to normal and let their mind wander.

- When you are ready, give them the suggestion to begin to let their mind wander on the play. The world of the play, the people of this world, their hopes and desires. Their fears and the obstacles in the way of their happiness.

- After a moment or two, tell them to let their mind focus in on the details of these stories, the images and moments their lives and world are made up of.

- When ready, tell the actors to imagine all of these images and ideas living in an ethereal cloud-like space in the upper atmosphere, ready to be called on for use at any time.

- Let actors know that when we draw upon this source, we do not have to plan for what images should come down, which images are right or clever or even make sense. All we have to do is call these images into the space and allow ourselves to be vessels for whatever shows up from our unconscious, connected to this larger spacious universal unconscious.

- Once they have grasped that initial idea, ask them to begin to draw down images and ideas from the play and call them out into the space. You may need to demonstrate by showing them yourself.

- Ask them not to question or judge any of the ideas, just to let them flow into the space.

- You may also have to guide/coach actors to be loud enough to be heard. Encourage them to share their ideas with the whole group. Tell the actors that if they hear an image or idea from another actor that resonates with them, they can and should repeat it, or reply to it.

Note: Repeating is the most valuable tool in this exercise so if no one is doing it at first, demonstrate by 'picking up' someone's good idea and repeating it. Chances are others will repeat your repetition. Maybe this will cause a chain. Or maybe someone will reply by saying something that the initial word inspires.

- When studying the play *Picnic* by William Inge, these are some of the ideas that actors began with:

  - Big blue sky
  - White apron
  - Heavy humid air
  - Sweat
  - Car radio playing an old favorite
  - A dock off a lake
  - The smell of a lady's perfume
  - Bare feet
  - Ice cubes in a glass of lemonade.

- As the exercise goes on, encourage actors to call out themes and metaphors as well as images. Also continue encouraging repetition:

  - Red convertible
  - Train ticket
  - Frustration
  - Attraction
  - Yearbooks with pages crossed out, torn out, missing
  - Red lipstick on a white collar
  - One white glove on a dirt road
  - A glass filled to the brim.

(continued)

(continued)

- Once themes and images are interspersed, ask for lines to be mixed in as well (if they are at a point in the process where they are somewhat off-book and know some lines to share):

    - If a woman's going to ask me to marry her, the least she could do is say "Please."
    - Mom, you don't love someone because he's perfect.
    - I'm only 19.
    - And next summer you'll be 20, and then 21, and then 40.
    - I'm never gonna fall in love.
    - I gotta get somewhere in this world.
    - Oh, Ma, what is it just to be pretty?
    - What's the use, Baby? I'm a bum.
    - You love me.

- Once the images begin to slow down, have the ensemble return to silent breathing to close the exercise. Once the exercise is over, circle the actors and have them discuss images that were the most meaningful to them as well as ideas that resonated through the group as a whole.
- Have the actors write these ideas in their journals for later use (this would have been very useful for my director who asked me to bring in gifts). Ways they can use these images could be:

    - Ideas for center images (Origin 5.5, Suitcase 5.6)
    - Ideas for personal atmospheres (Bubble 6.2)
    - Ideas for lines that a PG can be attached to (Refrain 6.1)

- Alternatively you can also hand out index cards/sticky notes and have each actor write meaningful words and phrases to:

    - Attach to their script for in-the-moment imagery during scene work (what images would go with what scenes?)
    - Put around their dressing room mirror for inspiration
    - Attach to a call board or butcher paper hanging in the space for group inspiration throughout the rehearsal process.

Coaching Gifts 2, Variations on Drawing Down the Play:

- Once actors have gone through the initial version of Gifts (which can be returned to many times throughout the process), feel free to add on variations. These variations could focus on what actors find striking or beautiful. Some of these variations could include:

- Drawing down individual characters (everyone draws down images of Madge)
- Drawing down a particular relationship (everyone draws down images of Rosemary and Howard)
- Drawing down the world/atmosphere of the play
- Drawing down the atmosphere of a scene (this is great before the first time you rehearse a scene off-book)
- Drawing down a particular moment in the play
- Drawing down the moment before the play
- Drawing down the hopes and fears of the characters in the play (this is lovely lead in to working on PGs).

Exercise 7.4 Upgrade

Based on MC's Tools Four Brothers, Qualities of Movement and Sensations

Many of us have played the theatre game 'Machine' as a part of our theatre training. Many times the game is used as a way to engage the actors in a physical ensemble-building exercise. The basic premise is this: one person goes into the middle of the room and begins a repetitive machine-like motion that engages their whole body, plus a sound. The next person must connect to the first in some way and

Actors engaged in 'Upgrade'.

Credit: Gordon Wenzel

their sound must be complementary (a bing when the other person's chuga-chug pauses, or maybe a high ratatat to complement the other person's low booms). One by one everyone joins the machine and at the end you have a larger machine consisting of the whole cast. Once they are in machine formation, you can ask them to slow down, speed up, grind to a halt or run out of gas. When getting used to machines, initially it is helpful to play a few times and encourage folks not to think too much and to just jump in and do the first thing that comes to them. The actors will be connecting with a kind of kinesthetic response and that is the training goal initially. Eventually the work can get more interesting by giving prompts. Prompts are great ways to really get people to take more risks and become more trusting of their initial ideas. Prompts can include:

- *Specific machines.* Make a toaster! A blender! A vacuum! (Encourage them to imagine all the associations with each machine, not just a realistic version—vacuum could be overwhelming noise, something gobbling, something running away from being gobbled, etc.)
- *Imaginary machines.* Make a homework machine! A doing the dishes machine! A taking out the garbage machine.
- *Seasons/holidays machines.* A winter machine, a halloween machine, a new year's machine, a 4th of July machine
- *Times of life machines.* A preschool machine, a middle school machine, a prom machine, a graduation machine, a wedding machine, a funeral machine, a nursing home machine, etc. (Remind folks that these don't have to be their experiences, they can just be what pops up! Again drawing down as we did in gifts, from the Universal Unconscious.)
- *Places.* Playground machine, hospital machine, library machine, beach machine
- *Emotion machine.* Rage machine, envy machine, depression machine, first love machine
- *Abstract color machines.* Blue machine, red machine, yellow machine, etc.
- *Abstract texture machines.* Crunchy machine, squishy machine, etc.

You could also connect any of these in new ways: squishy red rage machine, envy beach machine, winter wedding machine, etc.

Warning!

A reminder to stay safe and respectful is important at the beginning of this exercise. Have a quick discussion about what is okay and not okay. This could be different for each group but you have to agree or choose the most conservative if you feel some of your group are young or aren't comfortable expressing their wishes out loud. Example: "It is okay to connect by touching arms, hands, feet but not faces, not mouths, not pelvic regions, etc. It is never okay to hit, punch, pull or slap. You may think this a bit over the top but it is important if you are working in an academic atmosphere (or even if you are not) to create a safe space that protects everyone. Especially if you plan on employing rage, love, lust and other volatile machines."

Coaching Upgrade

Based on Chekhov's Ideas of the Four Brothers, Qualities of Movement and Sensations

Objective: Use the game of Machines to explore kinesthetic response in tandem with the four brothers of peak performance: a feeling of ease, a feeling of beauty, a feeling of form and a feeling of the whole, qualities and sensations.

Actors engaged in 'Upgrade'.
Credit: Gordon Wenzel

(continued)

(continued)

Coach:

- Upgrading Machine to include the Chekhov Technique can be done in a variety of ways:

  - Have actors use the *four brothers* when creating movements. Encourage them to follow the prompts above (or ones that you create) but to really focus on full body physical actions that have:

    - A clear beginning, middle and end (feeling of the whole)
    - A feeling of ease, even if they 'show' tension (the actor isn't tense, the character is tense—what is the difference?)
    - A feeling of form, ask actors to find new ways to connect—engage different parts of their body (especially if they are mainly using hands and arms), different levels, the space around them and each other or more than one person
    - A feeling of beauty (ask them to go deeper into their image, to not be satisfied with the first rendering but to follow the image and let it evolve until they are fully satisfied with it).

- Have actors create machines that respond to prompts with a *quality of movement.* Create a winter machine with the quality of flying, a summer machine with the quality of sculpting, etc.
- Have actors create machines that respond to prompts with a *sensation:* a falling wedding machine, a floating funeral machine, a tight-rope balancing middle school machine.

Exercise 7.5 Combining Gifts and Upgrade

Based on MC's Tools Four Brothers, Qualities of Movement, Sensations, Artistic Individuality and Jewelry

The combination of Exercises 7.3 and 7.4 can also be a very exciting way of physically exploring the imagery of a play, and take the exploration to the next level.

Coaching Combining Gifts and Upgrade

Based on Chekhov's Four Brothers, Qualities of Movement, Sensation, Artistic Individuality and Jewelry

Objective: To employ tools that engage kinesthetic response in tandem with tools for exploring and developing character.

Coach:

- After initially introducing both exercises (perhaps in previous rehearsals/classes or even in a longer extended class/ rehearsal), begin to create machines that utilize the images that the cast has drawn down. From our earlier example of *Picnic*, some ideas might be:

  - The new love machine
  - The quiet desperation machine
  - The lost train ticket machine
  - Missing clothes on the clothesline machine
  - I'm never gonna fall in love machine
  - The least she could do is say please machine.

Actors engaged in 'Combining Gifts and Upgrades'.
Credit: Gordon Wenzel

Another great way to engage the whole ensemble is to work together to explore character.

(continued)

(continued)

Coach:

- Begin by drawing down one to four characters in a Gifts exercise and then continue to explore these characters through upgraded machines.
- For this exercise, pull out the person playing the character to watch. From *Picnic*: have the other folks create a superficial/first swipe 'Madge' machine. Have the actress playing Madge observe the machine from all angles before letting the machine 'relax' or break down. I prefer the ending 'breakdown' to indicate the machine breaking down little by little because often times one word or phrase, sound or movement trails at the end of the piece giving it the feeling of a beautiful etude.
- Once the Madge machine is finished, ask them to go right into doing another Madge machine, a deeper one that deals with her hope and fears.
- If this gives you and the actress playing Madge sufficient inspiration stop there, but you can ask them for an even deeper third impression and this can often lead to some lovely revelations. Asking the ensemble to go past first impressions is important if you want to give actors something ultimately more useful than outward appearances.
- If the play you are studying has many characters, don't try to do them all in one day—the work can be exhausting, instead break them up into separate sessions. But always try to take the group through the character at least two times to avoid giving surface readings as the final expression for the character being examined.

Actors engaged in 'Upgrades and Gifts'.
Credit: Gordon Wenzel

The next natural progression of this is the relationship machine.

Coach:

- Approach this the same way as the character machines, by drawing down the relationship through a gift exercise to begin and then letting the group create the relationship while the two people playing the characters in the relationship sit out and watch.
- Continue through three renditions so you get beyond the surface reading.

One of the great rewards of these exercises is the crowdsourcing of inspiration for the actors. It takes the pressure off the leads to conjure the entire approach on their own (although they are certainly free to—the work only provides them more options) and it allows the minor characters to have a big part in creating the motivations and physicality of the leading characters. In short it allows everyone to tell the story together. This is also a great way to bring actors into the same play, by creating deeper understandings and connections to the world of the play and to the story they are telling as a whole.

Exercise 7.6 The Garden

Based on MC's Tools Four Brothers, Qualities of Movement, Sensations, Artistic Individuality, Jewelry and Form

Another great way to use the images drawn down by the Gifts exercise, or explored through Machine and Upgrade exercises is to take the next step and create a Sculpture Garden. Like Machine, many of us may be familiar with the acting exercise Sculptures. The idea is to have actors mill about the room (Milling and Seething) continually moving in and out of center toward the corners and outsides of the room. This is a silent exercise (at first). Beginning with taking in their breathing, then their bodies, then the space around them, then each other, ask your actors to begin to open their awareness and take in the world around them without the need to perform. The goal is to get actors comfortable with each other and with the space.

The instruction from there is to continue to "Mill and Seethe" or "move around" until a prompt is given and then each actor reacts to the prompt with a full body gesture.

Coaching The Garden

Based on Chekhov's Four Brothers, Qualities of Movement, Sensations, Artistic Individuality, Jewelry and Form

Objective: To use the ensemble to offer actors different options on physicality and character.

Coaching the Initial Sculptures:

- Using the images and ideas from Gifts, ask actors to move around the space, then take on a tableau (static forms) based on prompts that you call out.
- Offer prompts that at first are abstract (to lessen the actors need to perform for you or 'get it right') and then move up to the more complex.
- Push actors to use their whole bodies, engaging their legs and torso as well as arms, hands and faces.
- If you find their first renderings of any one image too literal, give the instruction that if you give a prompt more than once that they need to dig deeper and connect to the image in a different, perhaps more abstract way. This often frees the actors to try new ideas.
- As they get more comfortable with reacting to prompts, ask them to be aware and choose something they can hold with each prompt (not the standing on one foot tableau).
- Have them pause in one shape for longer and call out one actor to walk through the Sculpture Garden of the Images examining each one.

Coaching Variation 1, Documenting Sculptures:

- Give the actor walking through the Garden a real camera, and ask them to take three to five photos in the garden. The pictures can be full body or close-ups of hands, feet, faces, etc. Print these pictures later for use in any of the following ways:

- Attach to their script for in the moment imagery during scene work (what images would go with what scenes?)
- Put around their dressing room mirror for inspiration
- Attach to a call board or butcher paper hanging in the space for group inspiration throughout the rehearsal process.

- If they are already doing any of these suggestions with Gifts, this is a strong complementary addition. Documentation is also wonderful for any of the following exercises. Documentation can be done by anyone in the space, actors, observers, director, assistant director, stage managers, etc.

Coaching Variation 2, Partnered Sculptures:

- Have the actors leave the random independent walking and pair off. Pick an A and a B and alternate between the two—one as sculptor, one as clay. Be sure to demonstrate respectful sculpting by touching only what needs to move and what is appropriate. Demonstrating expression (yes, they should be sculpting faces) or shape as the sculptor is also helpful. Also remind the actors that this is a silent exercise.
- Give the prompts, allow the sculptors a few minutes to work with their clay and then to walk around the garden observing other sculptures based on the same prompt.

Coaching Variation 3, Group Sculptors:

- Ask partner groups to join other partner groups so that there are groups of four.
- Pick, or have them self select, an A, B, C and D.
- Run the same exercise but have three sculptors for each one piece of clay.
- They must collaborate silently and work together to create a piece they are satisfied with before they can observe any other team's work.

Coaching Variation 4, Group Sculptures:

- In the same groups allow there to be one sculptor for each prompt and use all three other members to create the sculpture.

(continued)

(*continued*)

- The clay can but does not have to be touching.
- Using the space or distance in the space is encouraged.

Coaching Variation 5, Ensemble Sculptors:

- Choose three to five people to sculpt the entire ensemble with a prompt.
- Working together and staying silent, create a sculpture with all the clay given.
- When the sculpture is complete, switch out the sculptors for other ensemble members and have the original sculptors become clay.
- Make sure everyone gets a turn to be on the sculpting team.

Coaching Variation 6, Master Sculptor

- Allow one person to sculpt the entire group.
- Make sure you have at least four different people act as sculptor if you don't have time to give the entire ensemble a chance to be the master sculptor. The reason for this is not that the chance to sculpt is so very important. It is important that each actor have at least three different opportunities to be a part of something big and filled with meaning. The big picture. That is the goal. If you have a strong conceptual statement or over arching theme, I would save it as a prompt until one of these last exercises, to really ground it within the ensemble physically.

Exercise 7.7 Beauty Quilting

Inspired by MC's Ideas on Higher Ego, Creative Individuality and Beauty

We as artists are fragile creatures in so many ways. We create beautiful meaningful pieces and then cannot resist the temptation to seek out approval on those creations. The relationship with the audience is a vital component of the performer's work but mitigating criticism is one of the largest obstacles an artist can overcome. Criticism is important, it keeps the work healthy and avoids self-serving goals.

Constructive criticism from gifted peers or brilliant novices can provide magical solutions when the work needs to grow. And it often needs to grow. But the biggest critic every artist is intimately aware of is the internal critic. The one that tells them their work is not strong, relevant or worthy. The critic that tells them they are a fake, that their work is 'less than.' One way I have found to combat this internal critic is to offer scraps of the ways in which others perceive you. Our internal critic often conjures images of 'what people really think of you,' a sort of paranoia of the psyche. When we ask others to share their actual perceptions, the paranoia loses credibility, strength and hold. This exercise is a lovely and simple way to deepen ensemble connections and release the hold of the internal critic by validating the inherent beauty each actor brings with them to the process.

Coaching Beauty Quilting

Based on Chekhov's Ideas of the Higher Ego, Creative Individuality and Beauty

Objective: To offer actors tools to negate or lessen damaging internal criticism and the power of the inner critic.

Coach:

- Before you begin, discuss with your actors the word 'beauty' in terms of how we approach it with the Chekhov Technique. Not just what is conventionally beautiful but that which makes a moment arresting.
- When describing people, share that we are looking to reveal an element of beauty that this person possesses.
- For this exercise we will be thinking of a one-line metaphor or element of beauty about the people we know. Pass out to each actor (you could also include stage managers, assistant stage managers, assistant directors and yourself—as long as these people are in rehearsal a majority of the time) a pile of index cards.

(continued)

(continued)

Each person should get as many index cards as there are people in your ensemble (including the extra folks).

- Have each person take these index cards home and on one side write the name of each person. They can decorate this name, write it plainly or print it—in such a way that it honors the person they are describing.
- On the other side a one-line metaphor that describes the person through imagery starting with the words: (Name) You are . . .
- Have everyone bring back these cards at a meaningful moment in the rehearsal process and seat everyone participating in a circle. (So Tina stands up and we go around the circle and every person in the ensemble shares their metaphor on Tina to Tina and the group.)
- Have every person take a turn by standing up and letting each person around the circle share their metaphor of the person to them.
- Then have the actors pass the index cards to the actor being described for them to keep.
- Samples of metaphors include:

  - Chris, you are a fourth of July picnic, comforting, joyful—with a touch of fireworks to boot!
  - Heath, you are moonlight in the woods, always showing us the way home.
  - Kelly, you are a warm puppy on a bad day, thank goodness for you!
  - Dustyn, you are a glamazon warrior princess in floral apron—fierce as all get-out, but prepared to bake should your friends need brownies.
  - Elaine, you are a pitcher of sun tea brewing on the porch, promising to be worth the wait.
  - Er-Dong you are a black swan in bevy of white swans, the standout among standouts.
  - Paula, you are an overflowing Halloween pillowcase of candy—a delightful mix just waiting to spill out.
  - Hutch, you are garden soil, helping everyone you meet to grow and take root at the same time.

Tips for Beauty Quilting

- *Tip 1.* Metaphors can be explained with a second sentence:

   Gary, you are the cherished photograph taped to my mirror—always reminding me of the beauty in life.

   Or remain mysterious

   Sherry, you are everyone's favorite pair of jeans.

- *Tip 2.* If you are out of time, as opposed to reading aloud, these can be delivered to each actor's dressing room table in an envelope. These make wonderful opening night gifts. Make sure all cards are turned into you first. Decorate the envelopes and make sure you read each of them before collating them. If any seem inappropriate or not right, you can ask the cast member to write a new one and be clear on what would be more appropriate. Reading aloud does, however, have the added bonus of the other folks in the cast reading and agreeing with the metaphor, which can add power to the message.

- *Tip 3.* If anyone is not getting along in the group, remind the whole cast that this is an exercise in beauty, it is up to each person to find that which is striking, arresting and meaningful about their colleagues. It is just as much about their ability to recognize and express beauty as it is about sharing their discoveries. The ability to recognize and express beauty is an essential component of the inspired actor's technique. The inability to do so reflects the inability to commit to the art form.

- *Tip 4.* You can have actors sign their names to each card or keep it anonymous—that is up to you. If there is any contention in the group, adding names is a good safeguard. If you are delivering instead of reading aloud, names provide a way for actors to thank their angels.

- Ways to use Beauty Quilting:
   - Create an actual quilt by attaching the index cards to a cardboard or poster board that everyone can see in the rehearsal

(continued)

(*continued*)

>   space or green room. Mix the names so that no two describ-
>   ing the same person are next to each other. Some can be
>   name forward, some can be metaphor forward. Have the
>   cast create the quilt as a group.

- Have cast members post the index cards around their dressing room mirror or in their acting journal.
- Meaningful times for ensemble members to present their beauty quilt patches include:

  - The last day of a class
  - The night before technical rehearsal start
  - The night before opening
  - Closing night.

- Beauty quilt patches can also be used at the beginning of rehearsal as a way for actors to explore character. Have each of the actors write a metaphor for each character (not just their own but all the characters). Remind them that this is a beauty exercise, they need to find the beauty of each character. After reading aloud in a group, give all of the cards to the actor playing the character.
- Another fun exercise is to allow the actors to create the cards as their characters—meaning this is an assignment given to the character. How would the character see the beauty in the other character? Their characters may be good or bad at finding the beauty in each other. These are nice posted because both the actor playing the character being described and the actor playing the character 'writing' the metaphor can benefit from the patches.

Exercise 7.8 Good Vibrations: Ritualizing Group Sound

Inspired by MC's Ideas on Ensemble

The next exercise seeks to incorporate sound and vocal work into the ensemble atmosphere. I like this exercise as a way to prepare for performance, really setting the tone vocally and putting everyone on the same page. The notes also evoke a very present moment-of-grace feeling.

Coaching Good Vibrations

Based on Chekhov's Ideas of Ensemble

By Samantha Norton

This exercise can be anywhere from fun to profound and is extremely effective for finding where sound travels and lands in non-traditional performance spaces. I don't refer to Good Vibrations as an exercise, rather I see it as proof that sound is tangible. Orchestras, bands and choirs are already aware of this because they train themselves to hear, feel and 'see' sound in a room.

Objective: To help your group 'see' sound as a real and powerful entity.

Coach:

- Assemble everyone into a circle.
- Ask your students to close their eyes as you explain this moment. You are going to ask that everyone to breathe easily.
- Tell them that in a few moments someone will lightly hum a note that is very relaxed.
- Once that person has hummed a soft and easy note, everyone else in the room will find that note and softly hum it.
- Then, without any planning or counting, someone will change that note up or down but relatively close to the first note.
- Everyone else then has the privilege to either stay on the first note or move to the other.
- Once this sound has been in the room, you can invite a third note to appear when the time is right and the same privilege exists for this: stay on the first note, go/stay on the second, move to the third.
- You can ask the students to change the hum into a vowel or voiced consonant. Let the sound live in the space for a while.

(continued)

(continued)

Then, just as you began without a designated leader, so will you end.

- Ask your students if they could hear a vibration or wave in the center of the circle. Could they attach feelings, atmospheres, colors, or shapes to the experience? Does the group vibration have qualities of Radiating out and/or does it feel like the sound is coming to you (Receiving)? Can this experience with sound vibration influence an actor's choice on creating the vocal qualities for their character? I think it can, and does.

In addition to using Samantha Norton's exercise to prepare for performance, another strong use of the work is to combine it with Exercise 5.1 Managing Mind Sweat or 5.2 Walking Meditation. The use of vibrations during meditation work is known throughout meditation communities as an effective way to quiet the mind and focus the attention. In yogic practice, one of the ways practitioners use vibration is through humming, known as 'Bhramari Pranayama' or 'Humming Bee Breath.' A simple sustained humming on each exhale offers a way of focusing the attention onto the breath by physically engaging vibration in the body.

Indeed when you are practicing this kind of humming during meditation (walking, lying or sitting), it can often begin to feel like it is emanating from your whole body and you can feel the vibrations resonate everywhere. A very relaxing exercise, this can also reset the actor's whole physicality and make voice a part of that physicality. When a group of actors are doing it together, the deeper meaning of yogic meditational practice also becomes clear. The meaning of the word 'Yoga' in Hindu religious texts is 'Union.' Whether you are engaging in a union with the divine through religious practice or engaging with a group of actors in an 'acting practice,' the result is the same—a stronger connection to the body, breath, voice and each other.

Exercise 7.9 Holiday Fun

Inspired by MC's Ideas on Ensemble

Instead of metaphors, another way to engage your cast in playful character exploration is to enlist the use of holidays and special occasions.

It doesn't matter if any actual holidays falls close to or on your rehearsals or performances, just the imagined idea of holidays will suffice. Holidays are nice ways to engage the actors with character work.

Coaching Holiday Fun

Based on Chekhov's Ideas of Ensemble

Objective: Use holidays to help actors play with character and build ensemble.

Coach:

- Assign homework to be presented in a rehearsal, have actors:
  - Create valentines from their character to another character
  - Create holiday cards from their character to another character
  - Create a New Year's 'photo card' to send to all their friends
  - Create a New Year's family newsletter to send to all their friends.

- Holidays themselves don't even have to be involved, just the idea of a special day. When appropriate have actors:
  - Write a secret admirer letter to another character
  - Write a Dear John to another character
  - Write an eviction notice to an adult child.

- Social media could also be employed:
  - Create a fake Facebook page for your character (all other characters should post on his/her page)
  - Create a fake Instagram for your character (all other characters should comment on his/her feed)
  - Create a chat thread with your character, be able to show/read aloud this chat with the ensemble
  - Create a Snapchat thread with your character, be able to show/read aloud this chat with the ensemble

(continued)

(*continued*)

- Create a fake dating account for your character: Tinder, Match.com, etc. and be able to show/read aloud this chat with the ensemble.

Note: All of these exercises should be taken as tongue in cheek. They are not meant to be deep character work. They are closer to the idea of Open Swim—playing with the ideas and themes of the play before having to manifest them. Keeping the process light and joyful throughout is a commitment to a feeling of ease and a feeling of the whole that can allow for a feelings of beauty and form. Let your actress playing Medea laugh with the actor playing Jason. Allowing them to laugh will help them to go deeper when they must roar with rage or keen with agony. It is like a strong psychological gesture. It begins in the opposite direction in order to make the fullest possible sweeping gesture to achieve its goal. If they must go there, allow them to go all the way.

Exercise 7.10 Angel Walk: Support for the Individual Performer

Inspired by MC's Ideas on Ensemble, Creative Individuality, Beauty and the Universal Unconscious

One of NMCA's most powerful exercises, the Angel Walk, can connect actors in ways that go far beyond traditional trust work. Indeed, my first time engaging in the exercise, with Mala Powers at the end of the tunnel, set me on the path to writing this book. Her simple recognition of me and of my work galvanized a desire in me to pursue this work more deeply and to work with these artists (and future MC artists) throughout my career. More than a decade later when I returned to NMCA for a refresher and once again took the Angel Walk, I heard the words Mala had given me prior to her death echo all around me in the new colleagues I had just met. It was as if she was there. And in some way, I believe she was.

Coaching Angel Walk

Based on Chekhov's Ideas on Ensemble, Creative Individuality, Beauty and the Universal Unconscious

By Wil Kilroy

Objective: To help each member of the ensemble to feel supported and appreciated allowing them to feel more comfortable going deeper into the work.

> This exercise is lovingly dedicated to the late Mala Powers, who found total joy within it, and her spirit is with me at every Angel Walk.
>
> —Wil Kilroy

Coach:

- Instructors/Directors set up a special place, creating an atmosphere of wonder and warmth. This could be done simply with a couple of strands of mini-lights, or perhaps LED candles, or more elaborately via projections of nature, and multi-colored patterned lights patterning the walls and ceilings.
- Soft inspirational music should be playing, or if there's a genre of music associated with the work of the ensemble, that might be another choice.
- Once the room has been established, the exercise is explained to the ensemble. It's an exercise in giving and receiving support—positive energy—from one another. Each individual can either remain silent, simply projecting good wishes to their ensemble mate, or they may choose to quickly whisper a positive attribute that the individual brings to the group, or a wondrous moment they've displayed during the working process.
- The ensemble is brought in silence to the prepared room and they form two lines, creating a corridor. At one end is a receiver—typically the teacher or director, with another teacher/director at the opposite end of the line as sender.

(continued)

(continued)

- One at a time, the 'sender' moves one of the ensemble members to the opening of the corridor and as they close their eyes, gently nudges them forward. The ensemble member walks the corridor, flanked by their peers, receiving the energy and support and possible verbal affirmations that they are given.
- Once they reach the end of the corridor, the 'receiver' gently replaces them into the line.
- Depending on the number of participants, the 'sender' can send others prior to the first actor reaching the end of the corridor.
- Once each individual has had a chance to walk through the 'hallway of support,' the ensemble exits the room, carrying the good energy forward into the next work session.
- Ideally this is done at the end of the day, and far enough into the group working together that they have had a chance to observe positive attributes which they may share.
- If a group is silent, that is okay too. Silent radiation can also be effective. However, it is rare that everyone will keep silent.

The Angel Walk exercise may seem simple but can be deeply profound if executed with integrity and joy. Consider incorporating this exercise at the end of a rehearsal process or class.

Advice from the Pros: The Power of Suggestion

By Karel Blakeley

It can be easy to slip into the mindset (and trap) that scenic design should provide a complete picture on stage. Show it all to the audience, the thinking goes, and they will be engaged, impressed and maybe even grateful for the holistic world on stage you've created for them. We're certainly accustomed to that approach in our theatres. And yet, one could argue that the more suggestive, minimal and metaphoric the scenic design is, the more immersive it can be for the audience. Instead of providing them with a novel or even a short story, why not give them a poem? Since most playwrights provide only a skeleton of a character on which actors and directors build,

Karel Blakeley, scenic and lighting designer, Le Moyne College.
Credit: Karel Blakeley

shouldn't designers take a similar approach to the worlds they create
on the stage?

Early in the twentieth century, the great American designer Robert
Edmond Jones, influenced by European designers such as Adolphe
Appia and Edward Gordon Craig, adopted and advocated a suggestive and simplistic approach. Both in his practice and in his writing,
Jones encouraged stage designers to think of themselves not so much
as architects or painters, but as poets. That is certainly sound advice
regardless of the configuration of the stage space. Rather than providing a complete picture, isn't it better to create an evocative minimalist
design that conjures up the world on stage with a few choice elements?
Like the few poignant words of a particularly engaging and touching
haiku poem, I think metaphoric suggestive scenery encourages audiences to fill in the blanks and engage more deeply because it pulls from
their own experiences and memories to finish the image.

I first became aware of how engaging minimalist scenic designs can
be early in my career when I designed a set for Kaufman and Hart's
delightful comedy *You Can't Take It With You*. For me it was a discovery born out of necessity. Written in the 1930s, the play takes place in
the cluttered Victorian home of an eccentric family. Although we were
working in a proscenium theatre, given the limitations of the budget
and crew, and the short build time, I decided that we should forgo the

walls and concentrate instead on designing and constructing ornate doorframes, wainscoting, and trim. To further delineate the walls, paintings and photographs hung in space below the large crown molding that framed and shaped the large room within the black masking drapes on stage. One night after the show opened, I overheard an audience member say how much the set reminded her of her grandmother's house when she was a kid, especially the color of the wallpaper. But there were no walls. She had completed the picture with her memories. It was a valuable and influential lesson.

Certainly a minimalist, sculptural approach to stage design easily lends itself to thrust or arena stages, black box theatres with flexible seating, and found spaces. In these less-dominant seating configurations, audiences view the work on stage more like a piece of sculpture in a gallery than a picture hanging on the wall. With viewers on three or four sides of the performers, sightlines are a more significant consideration. Substantial scenic elements like painted drops or box sets with walls, doors and windows that work so well within the picture frame of proscenium theatres tend to provide more interference than enhancement in these alternate performance spaces. In my experience, when developing scenery for thrust and arena stages, it's more important to create dynamic painted floor treatments; carefully place low pieces like platforms and furniture in the acting area; and hang units like beams, cornice molding and light fixtures above the stage. When taller scenic units such as drops, walls or doorways are incorporated, they are best placed on the periphery, around the outside of the seating or at the back of the stage, which can help to create a more immersive experience for the audience. And, like words in a poem that have multiple meanings, providing actors with elements that can be transformed by how they are used or juxtaposed can enhance the theatrical experience in these spaces. A large piece of white fabric hung up at two points can begin a scene as the sky, transform into a simple tent structure when one corner is untied, suggest ocean waves when billowed on the floor, and later cover a cradled body like a bed sheet or a death shroud.

Of course, some plays more easily adapt to thrust, arena, black box or found spaces than others do. It is difficult to take a door-slamming farce and have it succeed on an arena stage with seating all around, since timing and surprise encounters are keys to the action. Such plays survive and thrive on the solidity of the container. After all, birthday presents aren't much of a surprise if they aren't wrapped. So, early in the creative process, designers need to carefully consider how the characters come and go, moving in and out of the performance space. Are substantial solid architectural elements with doors needed or can the performers simply walk onto the stage? Or is it better to provide something more permeable so that actors may instantly appear anywhere through an opaque surface? For this purpose, drapes made up of narrow panels or strips of fabric can provide a versatile scenic solution, especially when hung on traveler tracks so that they can be opened partially or fully to reveal things like other scenic elements preset upstage. In addition, lighting drapes from the front or sides with a variety of colors and patterns is an easy way to convey a changing sense of place and mood.

The set I designed for a production of Shakespeare's *Tempest* at Le Moyne College's Jesuit Theatre, a black box theatre space with the seating arranged to form a thrust stage, illustrates how a minimalistic setting using drapes made up of strips of fabric as a background solved a number of challenges in the production. The director, Matt Chiorini, envisioned a dark and mysterious place, an island haunted by Prospero's revengeful magic. At the end of the play, however, he wanted the darkness to give way to light as Prospero departs the island, sailing homeward toward the setting sun on the horizon. As we developed the design, the primary scenic element on stage evolved into a large wooden disc that was raised up off the floor and sloped downward toward the audience. Performers could sit or step up onto the downstage edge, but since the back of the large circular deck was much higher, platforms at about table height near the back of the theatre allowed actors to exit off the disc left and right. In the center of the deck a large circular opening was cut, in which sat a black pool filled with water a little over a foot deep.

This was used on multiple occasions, like Caliban's waterlogged first entrance. Later, some of the downstage planks were removed to reveal an area filled with sand, suggesting a beach on the island. Wide strips of black, brown, deep green fabric and netting in a variety of textures and opacity hung across the back of the stage, touching the platforms at the bottom and running all the way up to the lighting grid 20 feet above the stage floor. Stretching across the theatre just in front of the top of this shredded drape was a dark wooden batten from which hung more pieces of the fabric so that they formed a border and suggested the swags of tree branches overhead. Smaller strips of the same fabric

The Tempest at Le Moyne College, W. Carroll Coyne Center for the Performing Arts, 2013. Set design by Karel Blakeley.

Credit: Karel Blakeley

were also attached at the edges of the round wooden deck to visually
anchor it to the black stage floor and the background. Ariel, Prospero
and other characters in the show could easily and instantly slip through
the strips of fabric, which were lit in various ways to suggest foreboding
forests and enchanted thickets. At the end of the play when all was happily resolved and Prospero departed the island, all of the fabric forming
the dark backdrop along the back of the stage split at the center, sliding
off to the sides to reveal actors holding a large ship's wheel and some
ropes silhouetted against a sunset in a deep blue sky. The circular sloped
wooden platform at the center of the stage formed the deck of the ship
and the fabric that hung on the batten above suggested furled sails. It
was a marvelous, magical transition and final image.

When working on a production in a thrust or arena-seating configuration, it is important to keep in mind that the audience becomes
increasingly aware of one another, of watching others and of being
watched as they view the performers moving about the space. In the
traditional proscenium theatre, there is not typically as strong a connection among audience members because they look over or through
the backs of other people's heads sitting in front of them. However,
the audience seated in a thrust or arena theatre, or within the intimacy of a found space is typically more deeply engaged in the communal encounter of the theatre experience. They are more likely to find
themselves paying attention to what others watching the performance

The Tempest at Le Moyne College, W. Carroll Coyne Center for the Performing Arts, 2013. Set design by Karel Blakeley.
Credit: Karel Blakeley

are feeling and how they are reacting. Scenic and lighting designers can
control this factor somewhat with the placement of scenery, and with
the angle and intensity of the lights, but the audience's self-awareness
is undeniable and increases their engagement in the experience. It's
important for the production team to embrace this altered viewpoint.

These thrust and arena seating arrangements tend to be more intimate, which provides the audience with a closer view of the performers
and stage. The choice and placement of smaller elements and details like
hand props and set dressing takes on a greater significance than is often
the case in larger proscenium theatres. And these objects can clearly
convey a sense of time period, place and social status of the characters
as effectively as larger pieces of scenery. A designer who provides an
actor with a delicate floral cup and saucer will alter the context dra-
matically by switching it with a battered tin mug. The audience looks
for and can find meaning in everything on the stage, and those things
that are not carefully chosen and thoughtfully placed or arranged can
confuse viewers.

Finally, in this minimalist approach to design it's important to only
add the things that the actors require for their work on stage, or those
things that assist the audience to better understand the context of the

world of the play and the characters. If it isn't used by the actors or doesn't communicate something about the nature of the characters and the place they inhabit, why put it on the stage? When less is more, the power and effectiveness of each thing placed on the stage is enhanced. Because of the significance of each of these elements, clear and frequent communication between the scenic designer, the production team, and the actors is especially important.

Like the author of the play, scene designers help write the story with the visual elements they place on the stage. And like poets, when they choose their 'words' carefully, they can help the audience revel in the power of suggestion.

Notes

1 Michael Chekhov, *On the Technique of Acting.* New York: Harper, 1993, p. 15.
2 Chekhov, *On the Technique of Acting*, p. 6.

Blood Wedding by Federico Garcia Lorca, adapted by Caridad Svich. Alley production directed by Anjalee Deshpande Hutchinson, lighting design by Heath Hansum, set design by F. Elaine Williams, costume design by Jenny Kenyon. Bucknell University 2009.

Credit: Enche Tjin

Credit: drawing courtesy of Pablo Guerra-Monje

8

CONCLUSION

Remember way back in the Preface when I said the first show I saw was *Annie*? Remember when I said it was on a proscenium stage? Remember when I said I *adored* it? Here's the real secret: non-traditional stagings often create exciting and innovative productions that connect audiences in magical ways, but non-traditional performance can be achieved *through any staging*. The exercises and techniques described in this book speak to a kind of meta-performance, performances that re-define what performance can be, and what they can mean to an audience. These kinds of performances already exist and some of them are on proscenium stages. They are the kind of performances that reach out beyond the stage and pull their audiences in. They are energetic performances, deeply inspired performances and are often peak performance experiences for those who perform in them and often for those who watch them.

Now I don't know if *Annie* was that kind of show, but it definitely had elements of that kind of engaging content. I know because I still remember them. I remember the choices the actors made and how they surprised and delighted me. I remember a choice an actor made in a performance 30 years ago.

Young audiences are not naive, they can smell you phoning it in. Sometimes it seems like it doesn't take much to captivate young audience members but this is a fallacy. In truth, what children connect to is the commitment they see from the artists. They don't need fancy

Non-traditional performance can be achieved through any staging.
Credit: Gordon Wenzel

What children connect to is the commitment they see from the artists.
Credit: Gordon Wenzel

production value or recognizable film stars in the cast. They want the
feeling of being asked into the world of the play. They want the invitation that can only come from a deeply dedicated actor and artistic team.
This may not feel like much, but it makes all the difference to those in
the audience of any age.

Many commercial theatre productions, which churn out shows on
a fixed timeline with little to no time for exploration and discovery,
often fall short on commitment. These are the shows that are 'nice.'
Polite. The ones that allow you sit back in your seat, with little tension
and little engagement. The shows are 'good enough' but not great. Not
extraordinary. The actors may be working hard, pushing out, but that
isn't the same thing as inviting us in. Many performers are trying too
hard because they have finished rehearsals and are in performance but
still haven't found something that feels just right—and they can't ever
fully commit if they don't feel like it's right. Or maybe the director felt
that it was good enough and didn't push. And maybe the actors knew

it was just good enough and that feeling undermined their ability to fully dedicate themselves to the choices they made. Chekhov saw this coming back in the 1950s. He wrote: "The theatre today is poor and the audience bored. It must be won with love and not fought."[1] Love for Chekhov meant a kind of communion with the spiritual nature of theatre. He had hope for the theatre of the future, believing it would eventually go in this direction:

> When I try to imagine what the theatre can and will be in the future (I speak neither in the mystical or religious sense in the moment) it will be a purely spiritual business in which the spirit of the human being will be rediscovered by artists. . . . I believe in the spiritual theatre.[2]

Here is where the exploration and discovery is crucial.

The Chekhov Technique encourages the actor to put the process in their own hands, strive to explore and discover that which makes the character vibrant and exciting in the actor's imagination and to do it physically. This kind of exploration can happen on any timeline and with any kind of director. It just requires the actor to commit to the pursuit of the extraordinary. When we are asked to deliver, this technique can offer a tangible way of pursuing the intangible. Chekhov stated: "The chief aim of my explorations was to find those conditions which could best and invariably call forth that elusive will-o-the wisp known as inspiration."[3]

Non-traditional stagings offer the most potential for creating pieces that strive to reach the audience in both tangible and intangible ways.

Exploration and discovery.
Credit: Gordon Wenzel

Actors, however, can create these kinds of relationships through sheer dedication to the form, the craft and the commitment, giving of the gift of meaning to the audience. Intention is a good start but dedication to building those creative muscles—to honing the instrument of body and its ability to relate and resonate meaning and allowing oneself full access to the glory of one's imaginative stores without judgment, criticism or fear—that is the job of the non-traditional performer. That is the work we have before us if we are to continue the legacy of the sacred communal experience that the theatre aspires to be.

Teachers and directors, if you have enjoyed and/or employed any of the tools and exercises in this book, I highly encourage you to pick up some or many of the titles listed in the bibliography. The works by Michael Chekhov are extraordinary and bring new meaning with each reading. They will become a valuable part of your library for years to come. In addition, other authors whom I have taken class with and studied from have also produced some excellent works that I highly recommend. In particular, Lisa Dalton's *SynthAnalysis* coming out in 2017 describes brilliant methods for directing inspired by the Chekhov Technique and methods that engage entire ensembles in a more imagistic meaning-filled approach to storytelling. Designers might also be interested in *To the Designer* by Lisa Dalton and Pablo Guerra-Monje on designing using the Chekhov Technique.

Lastly, I highly encourage you to attend a Michael Chekhov workshop, festival or class. The NMCA summer workshop is what I believe to be the best entry point for those new to the technique. It offers in-depth introduction to all of the main tools of the Chekhov

The sacred communal experience.
Credit: Gordon Wenzel

Explorations in imagistic meaning filled approaches to storytelling.
Credit: Gordon Wenzel

Technique while also providing a comprehensive guide to how they all fit together. They also provide strong pedagogy guidelines for those interested in teaching and/or directing students. MICHA is another wonderful resource for learning more about the Chekhov Technique. MICHA's work often focuses on specific tools and going deeper into those tools. MICHA festivals also offer wide variety of workshops to choose from so you can tailor your experience with them in a very personal way. Both NMCA and MICHA offer teacher trainings and certificate programs that are hugely useful if this is a technique you feel you will use often.

As our world grows more and more challenging in the face of diminishing human rights, clashes of cultures and a general lack of empathy, our work as artists has never been more vital, necessary and crucial to the future of humanity. Michael Chekhov saw the writing on the walls years ago. He advocated for a theatre of the future.

In an age such as ours when the trend of life, thought and desires is to become more and more materialistic and dull, the emphasis unfortunately is on physical conveniences and standardization. In such an age, humanity is inclined to forget that to progress culturally, life, and especially the arts, must be permeated with all kinds of intangible powers and qualities. That which is tangible, visible and audible is but a small part of our optimum existence and has little claim upon posterity. Afraid to leave the firm ground under our feet, we forever echo "Let's be practical!" Afraid to adventure and soar artistically, we sink deeper and faster into the ground we hold onto. And then, whether we notice it or not, and perhaps too late, we get tired of being "practical"; we suffer breakdowns, rush to (therapists)

. . . and periodically seek escape in cheap thrills, superficial sensations, swiftly changing fads and amusements . . . drugs. In short, we pay dearly for our refusal to recognize the necessity of sanely balancing the practical tangibles with the artistic intangibles.[4]

The pedagogy of empathy.
Credit: Gordon Wenzel

What effect do we have on our audience? What effect do we want to have?
Credit: Gordon Wenzel

Performance can heal. And so much of the world needs healing. What a great joy that this is our calling.

Credit: Gordon Wenzel

And yet Chekhov was ever hopeful. Mala Powers stated about Chekhov's vision for the ideal future theatre (or any performance) that it would "not confuse naturalism with realism" and could "entertain the public with diverse theatrical styles." In addition it would

> call for a sense of moral responsibility on the part of producers, directors, writers as well as actors. He said they must be willing to ask, "What effect will our production have upon the audience . . . Will what we are presenting have any positive value for them as human beings?"[5]

As we strive to commune with our audiences, grow empathy in our society, reveal truths in human nature and offer the sacred gifts of the intangible to lift aloft the spirits of our spectators, may we also seek to embrace Michael Chekhov's vision for the Theatre of the Future. Only then can we answer his call for a new kind of theatre and a new kind of art. Only then can we embody his hopes for his legacy, a new kind of artist. One that isn't afraid of the 'weird stuff.' One that can heal the world.

Notes

1 Michael Chekhov, *Lessons for Teachers of His Acting Technique*. Ottawa: Dovehouse Editions, 2000, p. 17.

2 Michael Chekhov, *Lessons for Professional Actors*. New York: Performing Arts Publications, 1985, p. 140.

3 Michael Chekhov, *To the Actor: On the Technique of Acting*. London: Routledge, 2002, p. 158.

4 Chekhov, *To the Actor*, p. 158.

5 Michael Chekhov, *On the Technique of Acting*. New York: Harper, 1993, p. 171.

Appendix

SHORT LIST OF EXERCISES IN BOOK ORGANIZED BY CORRESPONDING MICHAEL CHEKHOV TOOLS

1. Ensemble Work

    a. 2.1 Free Play/Open Swim, p. 24
    b. 7.2 The Revelation Spell, p. 202
    c. 7.8 Good Vibrations, p. 226
    d. 7.9 Holiday Fun, p. 228
    e. 7.10 Angel Walk, p. 230

2. Radiating and Receiving

    a. 2.2 The 'Here' Silent Story, p. 31
    b. 4.3 Project Your Energy, p. 101
    c. 4.4 Filling Space, p. 105
    d. 4.5 Bring Them In, p. 107
    e. 7.1 The Helpers, p. 198

3. Qualities of Movement

    a. 2.3 Sculpting in Space, p. 35
    b. 2.4 Voice Shapes, p. 38
    c. 3.1 Qualities of Movement, p. 52
    d. 3.2 Elemental Physicality with Music, p. 52
    e. 7.4 Upgrade, p. 213
    f. 7.5 Combining Gifts and Upgrade, p. 216
    g. 7.6 The Garden, p. 219

4. Archetypal Gesture

    a. 2.4 Voice Shapes, p. 38

BIBLIOGRAPHY

Campbell, Joseph. *The Power of Myth.* New York: Anchor, 1991.

Chamberlain, Franc. *Michael Chekhov.* London and New York: Routledge, 2004.

Chekhov, Michael. *To the Actor: On the Technique of Acting.* London and New York: Routledge (revised edition), 2002.

Chekhov, Michael and Mel Gordon. *On the Technique of Acting.* New York: Harper Paperbacks, 1993.

Chekhov, Michael and Deirdre Hurst Du Prey. *Michael Chekhov Lessons for Teachers of His Acting Technique.* Ottawa: Dovehouse Editions, 2000.

Chekhov, Michael, Charles Leonard and Nikolai Vasilevich Gogol. *Michael Chekhov's To the Director and Playwright.* Westport, CT: Greenwood, 1977.

Chekhov, Anton Pavlovich, Okla Elliott, Kyle Minor and Constance Garnett. *The Other Chekhov.* Fort Collins, CO: New American, 2008.

Chekhov, Michael, *Lessons for the Professional Actor,* edited by Deirdre Hurst Du Prey. New York: Performing Arts Publications, 1985.

Petit, Lenard. *The Michael Chekhov Handbook: For the Actor.* Abingdon, Oxon: Routledge, 2010.

Powers, Mala and Michael Chekhov. *Michael Chekhov on Theatre and the Art of Acting: The Five-hour CD Master Class: A Guide to Discovery with Exercises.* New York: Working Arts Library, 2004.

Stanislavski, Konstantin. *An Actor Prepares.* London: Routledge, 1989.

Zinder, David G. *Body, Voice, Imagination: ImageWork Training and the Chekhov Technique.* London: Routledge, 2009.

AUTHOR AND CONTRIBUTORS

Author

Anjalee Deshpande Hutchinson.
Credit: Bucknell University

Anjalee Deshpande Hutchinson

Anjalee Deshpande Hutchinson is a first-generation South Asian American who grew up spending time back stage when her parents acted, directed and 'prompted' for various Marathi plays during the 1970s and 1980s in Detroit, MI. Little did they know that the early exposure to theatre would influence almost all of her future career choices. (Surprise Aai and Baba!)

Currently, she is chair of the Department of Theatre and Dance at Bucknell University in Lewisburg, PA. As an Associate Professor, Anjalee teaches classes in acting, directing and devising. A graduate of the MFA directing program at Northwestern University and the BA theatre program at Kalamazoo College, her current focus is Devised Theatre and the Michael Chekhov Acting Technique.

Her background in devising includes training with Tectonic Theatre Project and also performing in four of their workshops productions. Her background in the Michael Chekhov Technique includes training with the National Michael Chekhov Association where she earned her teaching accreditation under Mala Powers, Lisa Loving Dalton and Wil Kilroy.

When she is not teaching, writing or directing, Anjalee can be found enjoying the craziness of raising her four awesome kids with her loving husband, Hutch.

Exercise Contributors

Pablo Guerra-Monje

Pablo Guerra-Monje studied at the Escuela de Artes Aplicadas La Palma in Madrid (Applied Arts in Sculpture) before attending Spain's Royal School for Dramatic Arts to study Scenography. He moved to the United States and earned his Master of Fine Arts with a concentration in Scenic Design at the University of Memphis (TN).

He worked at the National Hispanic Cultural Center in Albuquerque, NM, and The Santa Fe (NM) Opera. After teaching at the High School level in Santa Fe and in Portsmouth, NH, he joined the teaching staff at University of Arkansas Fort Smith in 2008.

Pablo has been awarded state, regional and national awards from the Kennedy Center American College Theater Festival. He has

Pablo Guerra-Monje.
Credit: Pablo Guerra-Monje

presented his work at the Prague Quadrennial of Performance Design and Space 2011. In addition, he was awarded the 2013–14 Prize for Innovative Teaching by the Association of Theatre in Higher Education and the Kennedy Center American Theatre College Festival, Region #VI.

Wil Kilroy

Wil joined New Mexico State University as Department Head of Theatre Arts from Maine where he was Chair and Professor of Theatre at the University of Southern Maine. At USM he directed dozens of plays and musicals including *A Midsummer Night's Dream* and *The Laramie Project*, which were invited to Kennedy Center regional festivals. Wil has worked nationally as an actor, with roles ranging from Steve in *Becky's New Car* to Laertes in *Hamlet*, and on TV productions such as *All My Children* and *Babylon Five*, and is an annual alumni guest artist with the State Ballet of Rhode Island. As co-founder of the National Michael Chekhov Association, Wil has taught nationally and internationally. Wil was awarded the Kennedy Center bronze medallion for achievement in Theatre Education in 2014.

Wil Kilroy.
Credit: Wil Kilroy

Samantha Norton

Samantha holds a Master's degree in Opera and Theatre from the University of Maryland, College Park, is an Adjunct Instructor for Bloomsburg University and Bucknell University where she teaches acting, stage combat, voice and dialect. Samantha has also been a guest instructor and director at Susquehanna University, Maywood University and the Pennsylvania Governor's School for the Arts.

Recent fight choreography include *When Push Comes to Shove* (a commissioned play by Professor Joseph Scapellato, Bucknell English Dept.), *Romeo and Juliet* (Susquehanna University), *Macbeth* (Blooms-burg University), *True West, The Wild Party* (Bucknell University), *A Midsummer Night's Dream, The Visit* (Pennsylvania Governor's School for the Arts), *King Lear* (Aulis Theatre, NYC), *Titus Andronicus, Twelfth Night, Taming of the Shrew* (Hudson Valley Shakespeare Festival, NY).

In addition to her fight choreography, Samantha has put her opera vocal training to great use as a voice and dialect consultant. Recent productions are *Carousel, The Mystery of Edwin Drood, Black Comedy, Pride and Prejudice* and *The Wild Party*.

Samantha received the New York Innovative Theatre Artists Awards for Best Supporting Actress in *How I Learned to Drive*. You can find

Samantha Norton.
Credit: Samantha Norton

Samantha's acting work on Nickelodeon's *Hi-Jinks!*, *Law & Order, Criminal Intent*, *Two Weeks Notice* and *Hitch*. www.samantha-phillips.com.

Essay Contributors

Karel Blakeley

Karel Blakeley is the resident scenic and lighting designer at Le Moyne College in Syracuse, New York, where, working alongside student crews, he has created sets for more than 60 productions. Professor Blakeley, who received his MFA in scenic design from Syracuse University, teaches courses in scene design, lighting design, stagecraft and *mise en scène*. He has also designed sets (and sometimes lights) for Syracuse Stage, Syracuse Shakespeare Festival, Cortland Repertory Theatre, University of Maine and University of Hartford in Connecticut. Over the years he has delivered numerous presentations on pedagogy and design at conferences for the Association for Theatre in Higher Education (ATHE) and the United States Institute of Theatre Technology (USITT). He compiled and edited *Projects for Teaching Scene Design* (Volume 1) published by USITT.

Heath Hansum

Heath Hansum teaches stage lighting, sound design for the theatre, computer-aided design for the theatre and entertainment technology in the department of Theatre and Dance at Bucknell University. His MFA in Lighting and Technical Production is from the University of Iowa and he did his undergrad work at Southwest Minnesota State University. He has been at Bucknell since 1994 and has served as the production manager for the Bread Loaf Summer Theatre in Middlebury Vermont since 2000. His work has been seen (or heard) at the Williamsport Community Arts Center, the San Francisco Opera, Williamsport Civic Ballet, Bloomsburg University, the Berkshire Theatre Festival, the University of Scranton, the Shakespeare Theatre of New Jersey, and is proud to be an artist affiliated with the Bloomsburg Theatre Ensemble. Heath has presented at conferences in the areas of the importance of a hands-on practical based education and safety in theatre. He was recently published in the text *Inspired Teaching*—a compendium of insights and techniques for teaching and is excited to be collaborating with Michael Gillette on his newest edition of *Theatrical Design and Production*. Heath would like to thank his wife DeAnn and his loving family for supporting his work and enduring his many late work hours in the theatre.

Lisa Loving Dalton

Lisa Dalton taught with the late Mala Powers, Chekhov Estate Executrix, for 18 years in Hollywood. They co-founded the National Michael Chekhov Association with Wil Kilroy, now offering the longest running Chekhov Training Intensive and Teacher Certification globally. Starting in 1980, Lisa studied with a dozen direct MC students and created the first documentary on Michael Chekhov, *From Russia to Hollywood*, with contributions to documentaries in the UK and Russia. Other DVDs include *Anthony Quinn's Life and Encounters with Michael Chekhov* and *The Michael Chekhov Actors Workout*. Author of the *Michael Chekhov Playbook, Murder of Talent: How Pop Culture Is Killing "IT"* and *Falling For the Stars: A Stunt Gal's Tattle Tales*, she created the first two of the Michael Chekhov International Workshops in America at the Eugene O'Neill Theatre Center in 1998 and

1999 that continue today as MICHA. She has taught in Moscow, London, Berlin, Paris, Brussels and around the United States. She also co-founded the International Michael Chekhov Association and the Michael Chekhov Studio, USA West. She is President of the Live Theatre League in Fort Worth, TX and on the SAG-AFTRA DFW Board. www.lisadalton.com www.chekhov.net

Ed Menta

Ed Menta is James A.B. Stone College Professor of Theatre Arts at Kalamazoo College in Michigan, where he teaches Directing, Theatre History, Dramatic Literature and Playwriting. Since joining the faculty in 1986, he has directed over 50 plays for Festival Playhouse of Kalamazoo College, including Brecht's *Threepenny Opera*, Josh Harmon's *Bad Jews*, Strindberg's *A Dream Play*, Sondheim's *Into the Woods* and Anna Deavere Smith's *Twilight: Los Angeles, 1992*. Professional directing credits include *Flyovers* by Jeffrey Sweet and *A Piece of Bone* by Aline Lathrop (BoarsHead Theatre in Lansing, MI) and *A Night in Praha* by Steve Capra, Michael Wright's *Shoulders* and *Fallujah* by Evan Sanderson for the New Playwrights Development Workshop in Chicago and New York (the last was the David Mark Cohen Award Winner and National Student Playwriting Award—Kennedy Center American College Theatre Festival 2010). Also in 2010, his production of Kalamazoo College alumnus Joe Tracz's play *Alison Shields* was invited to perform at the Kennedy Center American College Theatre Festival Region III, and received citations for original script and stage direction. From 2010 to 2015, he served as Co-Producer/ Artistic Director of the *Theatre Kalamazoo New Play Festival*, in which ten different Kalamazoo theatres came together to produced a dozen new plays annually in a little over 24 hours at the Epic Center in downtown Kalamazoo. His book, *The Magic World Behind the Curtain: Andrei Serban in the American Theatre* (Peter Lang Press, 1996), was selected as an 'Outstanding Academic Book' by *Choice*. His play *Mushrooming* was produced in New York in 2003 and published in *Healthy Primates and Other Plays: A Collection of Plays from the New Playwrights Development Workshop 2000–03*. Some of his essays and reviews have been published in *New England Theatre Journal*, *Shakespeare Bulletin* and *The Baseball Research Journal*.

Lynn Musgrave

Lynn Musgrave is an Oklahoma native, where she attended North-eastern State University in her hometown of Tahlequah, OK, major-ing in speech and theatre. She attended the University of Michigan on a Professional Theatre Program Fellowship, earning her Masters in 1977. Following graduation, Lynn remained another year in Ann Arbor as a senior acting fellow where she continued to develop her love of arena/thrust performing at the Power Center for the Perform-ing Arts. Arriving in Minneapolis in 1978, Lynn's first role was on the main stage of Chimera Theatre in St. Paul; a beautiful "mini-version" of the original design of the (sadly no longer with us) Guthrie thrust. Primarily an actress over the first five to seven years, Lynn worked with The Women's Theatre Project, Theatre in the Round (her favorite arena), and Park Square Theatre, where she made her directing debut. Lynn's directing and sound design credits over the past twenty-five years include such favorites as Flaming Guns of the Purple Sage, Jeffrey, Our Town, Long Day's Journey Into Night, and Power, to name just a few. Lynn has directed for Park Square, The-atre in the Round, Starting Gate, Chimera, Flying Pig, and The-atre L'Homme Dieu. On stage, Lynn's favorite roles include Dinah in The Dixie Swim Club, Martha in Who's Afraid of Virginia Woolf?, and Beatrice in The Effect of Gamma Rays on Man-in-the-Moon Marigolds. Lynn has been honored for her sound design, acting and directing from local to national levels; and she was named Theatre Artist of the Year in 2009 by Lavender Magazine. Lynn is a freelance voice talent and shares her Minneapolis home with her husband Bob Berglund, three cats, and five AKC Irish water spaniels.

Susan Picinich

Susan has been the Dean of the College of Fine Arts and Communi-cation at Towson University since June 2011. Her leadership has been characterized by a commitment to collaborative and interdisciplinary initiatives including a new Master in Arts Infusion and a move to imbed interdisciplinary arts and communication courses across the university curriculum. Prior to her appointment at Towson, she was Interim Dean of the College of Arts and Sciences at the University of Southern Maine and previously Associate Dean and Professor of

Theatre there for a total of 24 years in Maine. In 2009 she was a Fulbright scholar in Bulgaria, teaching at the National Academy of Theatre and Film Arts in Sofia. She has researched and presented on arts education in Canada, France, and Eastern Europe, comparing it to higher education practices in the United States. Susan currently serves on the Board of the Maryland Film Industry Coalition and the new Baltimore County Arts Guild. As a Professor of Theatre, Susan has taught Costume History and Design as well as other theatrical design and technical courses. She worked as a professional costume designer at Portland Stage Company, Maine State Music Theatre, and North Shore Music Theatre. She has also designed at the Walnut Street Theatre in Philadelphia and built costumes for Manhattan Theatre Club and Barbara Matera's Studio in New York City. She has worked on film costumes for *Signs of Life*, an American Playhouse Production, and also had minor assignments on the remake of *Sabrina* and *The Juror*. A native of New York State, she holds a Master of Fine Arts degree from the University of Michigan. From the State University of New York at Albany, she has a Master of Arts in Theatre History as well as a Bachelor of Arts in Theatre and French. She currently resides in Towson with her husband Stanley Max, a Lecturer in Mathematics at Towson University.

INDEX

Page numbers in italics refer to figures.

Taylor & Francis eBooks

Helping you to choose the right eBooks for your Library

Add Routledge titles to your library's digital collection today. Taylor and Francis ebooks contains over 50,000 titles in the Humanities, Social Sciences, Behavioural Sciences, Built Environment and Law.

Choose from a range of subject packages or create your own!

Benefits for you

» Free MARC records
» COUNTER-compliant usage statistics
» Flexible purchase and pricing options
» All titles DRM-free.

Benefits for your user

» Off-site, anytime access via Athens or referring URL
» Print or copy pages or chapters
» Full content search
» Bookmark, highlight and annotate text
» Access to thousands of pages of quality research at the click of a button.

REQUEST YOUR **FREE** INSTITUTIONAL TRIAL TODAY

Free Trials Available
We offer free trials to qualifying academic, corporate and government customers.

eCollections – Choose from over 30 subject eCollections, including:

Archaeology	Language Learning
Architecture	Law
Asian Studies	Literature
Business & Management	Media & Communication
Classical Studies	Middle East Studies
Construction	Music
Creative & Media Arts	Philosophy
Criminology & Criminal Justice	Planning
Economics	Politics
Education	Psychology & Mental Health
Energy	Religion
Engineering	Security
English Language & Linguistics	Social Work
Environment & Sustainability	Sociology
Geography	Sport
Health Studies	Theatre & Performance
History	Tourism, Hospitality & Events

For more information, pricing enquiries or to order a free trial, please contact your local sales team: **www.tandfebooks.com/page/sales**

 Routledge
Taylor & Francis Group

The home of
Routledge books

www.tandfebooks.com